Better Homes and Gardens®

CHRISTMAS
FROM THE HEART®

Better Homes and Gardens®

CHRISTMAS
FROM THE HEART®

VOLUME 10

Better Homes and Gardens Creative Collection™
Des Moines, Iowa

Contents

Holiday *Windows & Doors*

Deck the halls—and keep on going! Dress every inch of your home in holiday greenery and sparkle. Trim windows and doors with greens and wreaths to resemble festive holiday packages. Wreathlike in its delivery, this rectangle window is framed with magnolia leaves, topped with short-needle pine and sprigs of bright pepperberries, and accented with three silver bells hung from silken cords (below and opposite). The door frame (opposite) is a masterpiece of greens, combining pine boughs and cones, variegated ivy, pepperberries, and illuminated with white twinkle lights. Instructions begin on page 13.

*H*ave a ball with this sphere-inspired wreath (above). A faux fir base holds a bevy of red and white ornaments. The five central ornaments are painted different patterns—all in cheery red. A red-check ribbon winds its way though the wreath to end in a bow at the top. Hang this wreath anywhere—it's as fresh as peppermint-swirl candy!

Window dressing takes on a natural look. The faux evergreen sprig valance (opposite) is trimmed with hydrangea heads, twining ivy vines, and sprays of red berries. An advantage of using faux greens is that they can be placed near the fireplace, unlike real greenery. Built on a sturdy birch pole, this valance can be wrapped and stored to reuse the next holiday.

otton balls mimic tiny snowballs on a white and blue rectangle wreath (below). Start with a Styrofoam frame and add a snowy mound of cotton balls. Attach ice blue beads and an organdy bow for a dreamy wreath. A playful snowman joyously juggles snowflakes (opposite) Enlist help from your favorite little apprentices for both of these projects.

Dusty rose marries dusky green in this subtle, textural wreath (top right). You'll love the fragrance of fresh-cut Fraser fir. Dress it with metal reflectors, green faux berries, pepperberries, and green and pink swirling ribbon. Hang the wreath indoors or place it outdoors in a protected area. It will last for weeks.

Light and airy, this red and green wreath (bottom right) seems to float. Tie strips of green organza ribbon onto a wire frame to whip up this wreath in an evening. Attach a red organza bow and a big gold sleigh bell to enjoy ringing melodies whenever your front door is opened.

Pink and Green Wreath

Shown opposite.

YOU WILL NEED

Fresh 15" Fraser fir wreath
8 silver metal reflectors from
    antique Christmas lights (or
    candle bobeches)
8 small bunches of green
    faux berries
Sprigs of dried pepper berries
1 yard of 1½"-wide green
    grosgrain ribbon
1 yard of ⅝"-wide pink woven ribbon
Fine-gauge green wire

INSTRUCTIONS

Insert a small bunch of green berries into the center of each metal reflector. Referring to the photograph, *opposite*, wire the berry-topped reflectors to the front of the wreath. Center the pink ribbon over the green ribbon, then weave and wire the ribbons around the wreath; cut the excess ribbons. Combine the excess ribbons and make a single bow; wire the bow over the ends of the ribbons that encircle the wreath.

Attach a 6" piece of wire to each stem of dried pepper berries. Wire the pepper berries into the wreath, filling in the wreath with as many pepper berries as desired.
—*Designed by Patricia Church Podlasek*

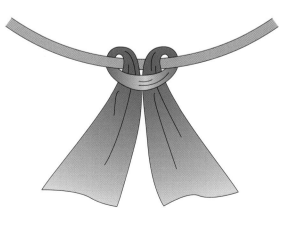

Ribbon Attachment diagram

Ribbon Doorknob Wreath

Shown opposite.

YOU WILL NEED

5"-diameter solid brass ring
6 yards each of two shades of
    2"-wide green organza ribbons
2 yards of 2"-wide red
    organza ribbon
2½" brass jingle bell

INSTRUCTIONS

Cut each shade of green organza ribbon into 9" lengths. Knot the ribbon lengths around the brass ring, alternating the shades of green. To knot the ribbon, fold a 9" length in half. With the ribbon under the ring and the fold outside the ring, bring the ribbon ends over the ring and through the folded end of the ribbon (see *below*). Pull the ends of the ribbon so the fold is snug against the ring. Continue adding all the ribbon lengths to the ring, alternating the shades of green around the wreath.

Thread the red ribbon through the top of the jingle bell. With the bell at the center of the ribbon, tie the ribbon to the center bottom of the wreath. Tie the ribbon into a four-loop bow; diagonally trim the ribbon tails.
—*Designed by Nancy Wyatt*

Lighted Doorway Swag

Shown on page 7.

YOU WILL NEED

2×¾" wood lath
Hand or power saw
Drill and drill bit
18-gauge wire; wire cutters
Glue gun; hot-melt adhesive
2—6' lengths of long-needle
    pine garlands
1—9' length of short-needle
    pine garland
Curly-leaf frosted ivy
Frosted bay leaves
Preserved bracken fern
100-bulb strand of white lights
    (with a brown cord if possible)
2 bags of dried pepper berries

INSTRUCTIONS

Measure the width of your doorway. Use this measurement to cut a length of wood lath wider than the doorway. To hang the door wrap, drill a hole 2" in from each end of the board and ¾" below the top edge. Thread a 12" length of wire through each hole and twist the ends together, forming a hanging loop.

Beginning with one end of a long-needle pine garland at the center front of the board, wire the garland to one half of the board, letting the excess drape down from the end of the board. Repeat with the second long-needle garland on the remaining half of the board. Center the short-needle pine garland over the board and wire it in place, letting the excess garland drape down.

Cut twelve 18" lengths of curly-leaf frosted ivy. Wire the ivy pieces into the garlands heavily at the top of the door wrap and lighter down the sides. Hot-glue the frosted bay leaves to cover the board and fill in spaces. Wire the light strand into the garland. Glue bracken fern into the swag. Glue in the pepper berries to add color.
—*Designed by Aubrey Dunbar*

Silver Bells Window Frame Wreath

Shown on pages 6–7.

YOU WILL NEED

2×¾" wood lath
Hand or power saw
Wood glue
Drill and drill bit
24-gauge wire; wire cutters
3 large silver bells
Dark red cording
Preserved magnolia leaves
Short-needle evergreen pieces
Small pinecones
Red berry sprays
Glue gun and hotmelt adhesive

INSTRUCTIONS

Measure the width and length of your window. Use these measurements to cut the wood lath to frame the window. Assemble the frame with wood glue; let the glue dry. To hang the wreath, drill a hole 2" in from each end of the top board and ¾" below the top edge. Thread a 6" length of wire through each hole and twist the ends together, forming a hanging loop.

Thread the silver bells on the cording, positioning each bell to hang at a different height in the frame opening. Wire the cording to the top center of the frame, securing the bells.

Referring to the photograph, *page 6,* hot-glue the magnolia leaves to the frame, completely covering the front surface and extending the leaves over the edges. Trim the evergreen pieces to lengths of 6" to 10". Hot-glue the evergreen pieces and pinecones between the leaves to fill in the spaces. Cut apart the red berry sprays and glue to the wreath.
—*Designed by Aubrey Dunbar*

Juggling Snowman Window Clings

Shown on page 11.

YOU WILL NEED

2 DecoArt reusable Styrene
   Blank sheets
DecoArt Black Leading
DecoArt Liquid Rainbow paint:
   Blue Cloud, Christmas Red,
   Crystal Glitter, Leaf Green,
   Primary Blue, Primary Yellow,
   and Snowflake White

INSTRUCTIONS

Peel the protective plastic off the Styrene Blank sheets. Place the sheets over the patterns *below* and *opposite.* Retrace the solid lines of the patterns onto the sheet with the black leading. Hold the leading bottle in your hand like a pencil, just above the surface of the sheet. Squeeze the bottle gently with even pressure. Reposition the sheet on the snowflake patterns to make as many snowflakes as desired. Let the leading lines dry for 2 hours.

Referring to the photograph on *page 11* and the pattern, *opposite,* as a guide, fill in the leaded areas with the paints. Be sure to fill in the entire leaded area with paint so the paint touches the leading and is even with the leading. For the carrot nose, fill in the area with Primary Yellow and Christmas Red.

Let the snowman and snowflakes dry for 24 hours or until the paint is transparent. Carefully peel the snowman and snowflakes off the sheets and press them onto a window.
—*Designed by Nancy Wyatt*

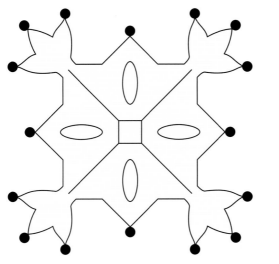

**Juggling Snowman
Window Cling**

**Juggling Snowman
Window Cling**

Red and White Balls Wreath

Shown on page 9 and below.

YOU WILL NEED

22 to 24" artificial pine wreath
STYROFOAM® products:
  5—3½"-diameter balls
  3—1½"-diameter balls
  6—1¼"-diameter balls
  14—1"-diameter balls
  1 piece of 1"-thick sheet
5 bamboo skewers
Round toothpicks
Painter's mask
100-, 150-, and 400-grit sandpaper
Tack cloth
Premixed patching plaster
Delta Ceramcoat products: Gesso,
  Sealer, and Gloss Exterior or
  Interior Varnish
Delta Ceramcoat acrylic paint:
  2—2-ounce jars each of
  White 2505 (WH) and
  Fire Red 2083 (FR)
Paintbrushes: ¾" wash, ½" wash,
  ¾" pouncer, #10 shader, and
  #5 round
Swirl rubber stamp
Paper towels
#2 wood pencil with unused eraser
4 rubber bands
Sobo glue
2 small plastic containers
Wire cutters
4½ yards of 1½"-wide red and white
  wire-edge gingham ribbon
Cloth-covered floral wire
Glue gun and hotmelt adhesive

INSTRUCTIONS

To make handles for the balls, insert one end of a skewer into each 3½"-diameter ball and one end of a toothpick into each remaining ball. Use the foam sheet as a drying rack, inserting the opposite end of the skewers and toothpicks into the foam. For safety, wear a painter's mask when sanding. Remove the sanding dust with a tack cloth.

PREPARE THE BALLS

Use your fingers to cover each 3½"-diameter ball with a thin even coat of patching plaster. Moisten your fingers with water and smooth out the plaster. Let the plaster dry. Sand the plaster-covered balls with 100- and then 150-grit sandpaper until the surface is smooth.

Using a ¾" wash brush, apply a coat of gesso to each plaster-covered ball. Let the gesso dry completely. Sand the balls with 150-grit sandpaper. Use a ¾" wash brush to apply a coat of sealer. When the sealer is dry, sand the balls with 400-grit sandpaper.

PAINT THE BALLS

Using a ¾" wash brush and WH, base-coat all the 3½" balls. Let the paint dry.

For one 3½" ball, brush the swirl rubber stamp with FR paint. To remove excess paint, gently tap the stamp on a paper towel. Stamp the image on the ball, carefully rocking the stamp on the curved surface without changing the position. Repeat to randomly stamp swirls over the ball, reapplying paint to the stamp after each impression.
For the 3½" FR polka-dot balls, use a ¾" pouncer to make large dots and the eraser end of a pencil to make small dots. Dip the pouncer or eraser into the paint; touch the paint to the surface of the ball. Repeat to make random dots over the ball, dipping in paint before each dot.

For the 3½" check ball, draw intersecting horizontal and vertical pencil lines around the ball the width of the #10 shader. Select one side of the ball for the front. Load the shader with FR and, referring to the photograph for guidance, paint every other square for a checkerboard design.

To make the 3½" striped ball, place rubber bands around the ball to create eight equal sections. Using the rubber bands as a guide, use a pencil to lightly draw the section lines. Remove the rubber bands. Use a #5 round brush and FR to paint every other section.

When the paint is completely dry, use the ¾" wash brush to apply a coat of varnish to each 3½" ball. Let the varnish dry. Trim off or remove the skewers.

Using a ½" wash brush and WH, base-coat one 1½"-diameter ball, three 1¼"-diameter balls, and three 1"-diameter balls. Using a ½" wash brush and FR, base-coat two 1½"-diameter balls, three 1¼"-diameter balls, and 11—1"-diameter balls.

When the paint is completely dry, sand with 400-grit sandpaper. Make a mixture using 4 tablespoons each of WH and Sobo glue. Holding onto the toothpick, dip each WH ball into the mixture to completely cover the ball. Dip the balls 3 or 4 times in the mixture until the surface is smooth, letting the mixture dry after each layer. Repeat with a mixture of FR and Sobo glue for the red balls.

When the final layer is completely dry, use the ½" wash brush to apply a coat of varnish to each mixture-coated ball. Let the varnish dry. Use the wire cutters to trim off the protruding toothpicks.

ASSEMBLE THE WREATH

From the 1½"-wide gingham ribbon, cut a 2-yard length for the bow and an 18" length for the tails. Use the ribbon lengths and 12" of the floral wire to make an 8-loop bow with a center knot. Position the bow on the wreath at the center top and secure with the floral wire. Cut Vs in the ends of the ribbon tails.

Arrange the balls on the wreath, referring to the photograph *opposite* or on *page 9*. When pleased with the arrangement, hot glue the balls to the wreath. Beginning and ending under the bow, weave the remaining gingham ribbon around the wreath, wiring it in place as desired.

For a hanging loop, fold a piece of cloth-covered floral wire in half. Secure the ends to the center back of the wreath.

—*Designed by Annabelle Keller*

Snowball Wreath

Shown on page 10.

YOU WILL NEED

10×12" Styrofoam rectangle
2 bags of cotton balls
Crafts glue
Light blue pearls
3½ yards of 1⅜"-wide light blue organza ribbon

INSTRUCTIONS

Draw a 6½×8½" rectangle centered on one side of the foam. Cut on the drawn lines, removing the center to create a rectangle opening.

Glue cotton balls on the foam frame, completely covering the front and sides of the wreath, including the edges of the center opening. Glue light blue pearl beads between the cotton balls. Let the glue dry.

Cut a 90" length of light blue organza ribbon. Tie the ribbon into a six-loop bow around the center bottom of the wreath. Diagonally trim the ribbon tails. For the hanging loop, bring the remaining ribbon around the center top of the wreath; knot the ends together.

—*Designed by Carrie Topp*

Red Berry and Vine Window Swag

Shown on page 8 and above.

YOU WILL NEED

Birch pole
22-gauge wire
Wire cutters
Long-needle pine garland with pinecones
Frosted grape leaf bush
24" berry sprays
Dried hydrangea heads
Glue gun and hotmelt adhesive

INSTRUCTIONS

Use a length of birch pole that is about the width of your window. To hang the topper, cut two 12" lengths of wire. Use the wire to make a hanging loop about 6" in from each end of the pole.

Wire the long-needle pine garland to the pole. Cut apart the frosted grape leaf bush and wire the pieces into the garland, creating an asymmetrical design. Attach the berry sprays with wire. Glue the hydrangea heads to the topper with hotmelt adhesive.

—*Designed by Aubrey Dunbar*

Paper Perfection

Transform paper pieces into textured packages, gift holders, greeting cards, journal covers, and ornaments. Use stamping and embossing tools to wrap the holidays in style. A take-out-style box (right) is hand-embossed, gilded in gold, and topped elegantly with a swirl of red wire-edge organza ribbon. Instructions start on page 25.

*G*ive a present with presence by making your own gift boxes (opposite and above). Using rubber stamps with distinctive designs, you can design glittery or textural boxes that will be equally as treasured as the gifts they hold. Embellish the boxes with ribbon, yarn, and pine needles for a truly custom look.

Pack a puffy pillow box (above) with sweet treats for the occasion. Scrapbooking papers and card stock are put to use in perfectly sized small containers. Topped with a wire-wrapped polished stone, the gift is complete.

*R*ecord all your holiday addresses and memories in a handmade address book and matching journal (above left). Decorate kraft-paper covers with a reindeer rubber stamp and sentimental collage materials, such as pieces of ribbon or lace, snippets of paper, colorful cancelled stamps, and charms.

If metalworking isn't on your list of skills, don't despair. Embossed and stamped gold ornaments (above right) are a snap to make—without lifting a hammer! Choose your favorite holiday motif—a proud reindeer, for example—or combine a variety of seasonal snowflakes, stars, or holly to style your greeting.

*Create distinctive holiday greeting cards,
with card stock, stamps, ink, photos, ribbon—
and your own sense of holiday fun and creativity.*

*G*et handy for the holidays! Paper-crafted gift gloves (left) require only basic rubber-stamping skills. A ribbon at the back allows you to hang your gift anywhere, and the coordinating hand-stamped gift card is a smart finish. Dangle gloves from the mantel alongside Christmas stockings for a lustrous holiday statement.

Glove Gift Holder

Shown opposite.

YOU WILL NEED

2—8½×11" sheets of white card stock

Accu-Cut Roller Die Cutting System and Dies: Jumbo Glove G1355 and Small Gift Tag T1123, or tracing paper and medium-hole punch

Inkadinkado Daydreams rubber stamps: Holiday Tile Collage 8404 and Borderline 8391

ColorBox pigment stamp pads: Dusty Plum and Gold

ColorBox Metalextra stamp pad: Verdigris

Permanent paper glue

Glitter

20" length of ⅜"-wide dusty rose ribbon

Clear embossing powder

Embossing heat tool

4" length of fine gold cord

INSTRUCTIONS

Use the die-cutting machine and Accu-Cut Dies to cut two gloves and one gift tag from the white card stock. Or trace the glove patterns to make a complete glove, and the gift tag pattern, onto tracing paper. Cut out the patterns. Trace two gloves and one gift tag onto the white card

stock; cut out the shapes. Punch holes in the gloves at the center of each scallop.

For the front glove, rub Dusty Plum ink onto one side of a glove; let the ink dry. Ink the Holiday Tile Collage stamp with Verdigris ink and

stamp the image onto the Dusty Plum-rubbed glove. Repeat to fill the front glove, reinking the stamp after each impression. Let the ink dry. Apply a thin coat of glue to the top 1" of the stamped glove. Immediately sprinkle glitter over the glue. Let the glue dry. Glue the two gloves together, leaving the top edge open. Thread the ribbon through one of the back scallops, and tie the ends into a bow.

Ink the Borderline stamp with gold ink and stamp the image onto the gift tag. While the ink is wet, sprinkle it with clear embossing powder. Tilt the paper on edge and tap off the excess powder. Use the heat tool to melt the powder, creating a shiny raised image. Personalize the gift tag with the recipient's name. Use the fine gold cord to tie the gift tag to the glove.

—Designed by Dawn Houser

Stamped Glove Gift Card

© 2001 Accu-Cut® Systems

Stamped Glove Gift Holder
Cut 2 on solid lines

© 2001 Accu-Cut® Systems

Embossed Holiday Collage and Reindeer Ornaments

Shown on page 22 and below.

YOU WILL NEED

For each ornament:
Gold ColorBox pigment stamp pad
Suze Weinberg's Gold Ultra Thick
Embossing Enamel
Paper plate
Embossing heat tool
Tiny clear holeless beads
Plastic container
¼"-wide double-side crafter's tape
Crafts glue

For holiday collage ornament:
3¼×4¼" piece of white mat board
Inkadinkado Daydreams rubber
stamp, Holiday Tile Collage 8404
5" length of ⅝"-wide ribbon with
a gold edge

For reindeer ornament:
2×3¼" piece of white mat board
Inkadinkado Daydreams rubber
stamp, Reindeer 8411
3½" length of ¼"-wide black
satin ribbon

INSTRUCTIONS

Ink one side of the mat board in gold by rubbing it with the stamp pad. Sprinkle gold embossing enamel over the entire inked surface of the mat board. Tap off the excess embossing enamel on a paper plate. Heat the embossing enamel with the heat tool until it melts. Repeat the process two more times until the surface is as smooth as glass.

Immediately ink the stamp with gold ink and press it into the still-warm embossing enamel. Hold the stamp in place for 60 seconds and lift it up gently. The image will be embedded into the embossed surface.

Pour the tiny clear beads into a plastic container. Apply the double-side crafter's tape to the edges of the ornament and dip the edges into the bowl of beads.

For the hanging loop, fold the ribbon in half. Overlap and glue the ribbon ends to the top center on the back of the ornament.
—*Designed by Dawn Houser*

Reindeer Card

Shown on page 23.

YOU WILL NEED
4¼×11" rectangle of white
card stock
1⅞×3½" rectangle of gold paper
1⅝×3¼" rectangle of cream
card stock
Inkadinkado Daydreams rubber
stamps: Pine Sprig 8419,
Reindeer 8411, and Merry
Little Christmas 8410
Honeydew-colored Tsukineko Encore
Ultimate Metallic stamp pad
Quicksilver-colored ColorBox
Metalextra stamp pad
Tsukineko Ultimate Metallic Gel
pens: green and red
Glue stick

INSTRUCTIONS

For the card, fold the 4¼×11" rectangle of white card stock in half to measure 4¼×5½". Ink the Pine Sprig stamp with Honeydew and randomly stamp the image onto the front of the card, reinking the stamp after every one or two impressions. Let the images dry.

Ink the Reindeer stamp with Quicksilver and stamp the image on the center of the cream card stock. Let the image dry. Mount the stamped cream card stock centered on the gold paper with the glue stick, creating a ⅛" gold border. Mount the gold/stamped card stock layers centered on the front of the card.

Use the green and red gel pens to embellish the wreath on the reindeer. Ink the Merry Little Christmas stamp with Quicksilver and stamp the image inside the card.
—*Designed by Dawn Houser*

Folded Photo-Mount Card

Shown on page 23.

YOU WILL NEED

4¼×11" rectangle of white card stock

Inkadinkado Daydreams rubber stamp, Snow Post Collage 8420

ColorBox pigment stamp pads: Black, Peony, and Moss Green

Black embossing powder

Embossing heat tool

Metallic gold ink pad

Micro-hole punch

Mini-grommets

Double-side tape and photo

16" length of ½"-wide rose ribbon

INSTRUCTIONS

Lightly draw a line across the card stock 2¾" from each short edge. Fold the card stock on the drawn lines, creating a 4¼×5½" card with two flaps that meet at the center front.

Ink the Snow Post Collage stamp with black ink and stamp the image onto the front of the flaps. Repeat to fill the front flaps, reinking the stamp after each impression. While the ink is wet, sprinkle it with black embossing powder. Tilt the paper on edge and tap off the excess powder. Use the heat tool to melt the powder, creating a shiny raised image.

Unfold the card. Ink the Snow Post Collage stamp with black ink and repeatedly stamp the image to fill the inside of the card, reinking the stamp after each impression. Let the images dry.

Rub Peony and Moss Green ink into different areas of the embossed designs on the front of the flaps until the flaps are filled with color. Let the ink dry. Lightly rub metallic gold ink randomly onto the front flaps.

Punch a hole, centering it a scant ¼" from the center edge of each flap. Apply the grommets. Mount the photo inside the card with double-side

tape. Thread the ribbon through the grommets, tie into a bow, and trim the ends at an angle.
—*Designed by Dawn Houser*

Winter Memories Journal and Address Book

Shown on page 22 and right.

YOU WILL NEED

For each book:

Red Castle reindeer rubber stamp

Ranger Big & Juicy Rainbow dye ink pad: Spice

Deckle-edge scissors

Glue stick

Gel pens: white and gold

For the journal:

6×8" blank journal with kraft paper cover

Card stock: oatmeal speckle, white, and 4¼×5½" rectangle of medium green

3×4" Magic Stamp embossable foam block

3×4" piece of lace or embroidery

Embossing heat tool

Metallic braid and chenille needle

40" length of 1¼"-wide sheer ribbon

Collage materials, such as canceled stamps, buttons, and charms

Gem glue, if embellishing with buttons or charms

For the address book:

3×4" address book with kraft paper color cover

Card stock: oatmeal speckle and deep green

22" length of ⅛"-wide grosgrain ribbon

JOURNAL

Ink the reindeer stamp with Spice ink, positioning the stamp on the desired area of the stamp pad. Stamp the image onto the oatmeal speckle card stock. Let the image dry.

Use the deckle-edge scissors to cut around the stamped image, creating a ⅜" border. Mount the stamped

oatmeal speckle card stock on the white card stock with the glue stick. Use the deckle-edge scissors to cut the white card stock 1⁄16" beyond the edges of the oatmeal speckle card stock.

Emboss the Magic Stamp block with the pattern texture from the piece of lace, following the manufacturer's instructions. Using the olive/green area of the ink pad, stamp the image onto the medium green card stock. Repeat to fill one side of the card stock, reinking the stamp after each impression. Let the images dry.

Mount the white bordered reindeer centered on the stamped side of the medium green card stock with the glue stick. Use the white gel pen to color the reindeer and stars. Thread the needle with metallic braid and make three straight stitches across the narrow stamped border on the left and right edges of the stamped image.

With the center of the ribbon on the spine of the journal, bring the ribbon ends around to the opposite edge and tie into a bow.

With the center of the ribbon on the spine of the journal, bring the ribbon ends around to the opposite edge and tie into a bow. Mount the layered card stock centered on the front of the journal with the glue stick, securing the ribbon to the front

cover. Glue stamps and buttons to the front cover.

ADDRESS BOOK

Ink the reindeer stamp with Spice ink, positioning the stamp on the desired area of the stamp pad. Stamp the image onto the oatmeal speckle card stock. Let the image dry.

Use the deckle-edge scissors to cut around the stamped image, creating a $1/16"$ border. Mount the stamped oatmeal speckle card stock on the deep green card stock with the glue stick. Use the deckle-edge scissors to cut the deep green card stock $1\frac{1}{16}"$ beyond the edges of the oatmeal speckle card stock.

Use the white gel pen to color the reindeer and stars. Add fine lines in the inner border of the image with white and gold gel pens.

With the center of the ribbon on the spine of the address book, bring the ribbon ends around to the opposite edge and tie into a bow. Mount the green bordered reindeer centered on the front of the book cover with the glue stick, securing the ribbon to the front cover.
—*Designed by Judi Kauffman*

Gift Boxes
Shown on pages 19–21 and above.

YOU WILL NEED
For all gift boxes:
Tracing paper
Additional box templates (optional)
Patterned scrapbook paper, hand-made paper, or card stock
Crafts knife, metal straightedge, and cutting mat
Scissors
Scoring tool
Double-stick adhesive sheet
Crafts glue
Assorted embellishments, such as ribbon, cord, wire, smooth stones, pine needles, and yarn
For heat embossing:
Texture-pattern rubber stamp
Clear embossing ink pad
Verdigris embossing powder
Embossing heat tool
For hand-press embossing:
Hand-press-style embossing tool
Gold rub-on

INSTRUCTIONS

Trace the pillow box pattern *opposite* onto tracing paper, including the score lines; cut out. To change the size of the pillow box, enlarge or reduce the entire pattern on a copy machine, or lengthen or shorten the box (see the small pillow box *left*). In addition, templates are available for a variety of boxes, including the rectangular box and carry-out carton (see Sources, *page 158*).

Experiment with a variety of papers to create boxes. To use lightweight paper, adhere it to thin card stock before tracing the pattern. Try different embossing techniques on the papers. For a look similar to the small pillow box, heat-emboss a patterned paper using a textured rubber stamp, clear embossing ink, and verdigris embossing powder. Or, before scoring the paper, use a squeeze-type embossing tool to emboss the paper. After the box is assembled, lightly buff the raised areas and edges of the box with gold rub-on (see the carry-out carton on *page 19*).

Trace the pattern onto the back of the paper or card stock. Cut out the shape on the solid lines. Very lightly score the pieces on the dotted lines. Fold the pieces along the score lines. Glue the flaps and let the glue dry.

Place the gift in the box and close the flaps. Wrap ribbon around the box and tie a bow at the top, or wrap strips of papers around the box. Embellish the box with paper cutouts, a wire-wrapped stone, or paper-wrapped pine needles secured with yarn.
—*Designed by Judi Kauffman*

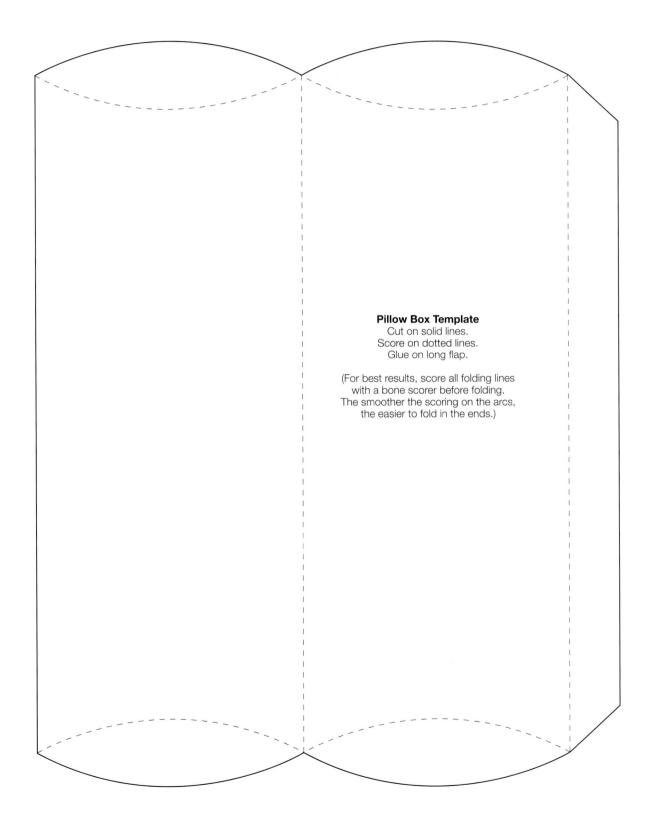

Pillow Box Template
Cut on solid lines.
Score on dotted lines.
Glue on long flap.

(For best results, score all folding lines
with a bone scorer before folding.
The smoother the scoring on the arcs,
the easier to fold in the ends.)

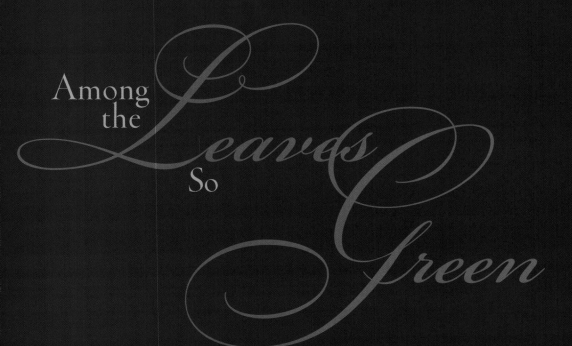

Among the Leaves So Green

Pick the traditional choice for holiday decor—fresh-cut greenery. Ancient cultures used holly, evergreen, and ivy to decorate because the sprigs remained verdant during the long, cold winters. These holiday favorites symbolized everlasting good luck. Your good luck is that these holidays arrangements are easy to make. Hang a kissing ball (opposite) and get ready to pucker up! The traditional ivy-and-holly-covered ball, suspended above a holiday table, an archway, or a doorway, will last all through the holidays. Instructions start on page 36.

Serve a holiday-hue centerpiece with lacy baby's breath, two-tone holly leaves, and bright red roses (opposite). Start with an oasis foam base centered on a cake pedestal and build layers of blooms. Surround the arrangement with glowing, lighted votives for a sparkling touch.

A cheery red, white, and green plaid table runner unites the season's colors perfectly. Weave velvet or satin solid color ribbons with satin plaid ribbons into a striking base that anchors your holiday centerpiece. Bold red and green tassels add to the elegance.

*L*ike a soft blanket of snow that warms the base of an evergreen tree in the forest, a tree skirt placed beneath the tree in your home provides a foundation for the bounteous gifts you give and receive. Overlapping red and green fabric squares, edged in plaid ribbon and trimmed with tassels, make this stylish skirt (above) a breeze to assemble. Beautifully handmade velvet-embossed boxes complement the satiny tree skirt. Tuck a few under the tree until you offer them as hostess gifts or use them to store holiday trims.

Soft, shiny cones filled with sweetheart roses and greenery (opposite) bring added freshness to your tree. Woven from velvet and satin ribbons, the cones can hold a variety of seasonal trims or treats.

Holly-and-Ivy Kissing Ball

Shown on page 31 and below.

YOU WILL NEED
5" foam ball
Fresh or silk ivy
Fresh or silk holly
U-shape pins
3½ yards of 1"-wide red
   plaid ribbon

INSTRUCTIONS

Note: Use fresh holly and ivy only if you plan to use your kissing ball for a single day.

Cut an 18" length of ribbon for the hanger. Glue and pin the hanging loop to the top of the foam ball. Cut assorted lengths of holly and ivy. Use U-shape pins to hold the holly and ivy to the foam ball.

With the remaining ribbon, tie a eight-loop bow and trail the ends through the decorated ball, pinning the ribbon in place.

Fresh Holly and Roses "Cake" Centerpiece

Shown on page 32.

YOU WILL NEED
Glass or crystal pedestal cake dish
Florist's foam and clay
1 or 2 bunches of red
   sweetheart roses
Fresh holly
Baby's breath for filler

INSTRUCTIONS

Cut florist's foam and mount it on the center of the pedestal cake dish. Soak the foam thoroughly in water.

Cut rose stems to about 3" in length. Insert the rose stems into the florist's foam, spacing the roses about 3" apart.

Cut holly into short pieces, and insert into the foam between the roses. Cut short pieces of baby's breath to fill in empty spaces.

Water the arrangement twice a day and it should last about a week.

Woven Ribbon Table Runner

Shown on pages 32–33 and opposite.

YOU WILL NEED
1¼ yards of 22"-wide fusible
   nonwoven firm interfacing
Fabric marking pencil
8 yards of 1½"-wide red
   plaid ribbon
9½ yards of ⅝"-wide red
   velvet ribbon
9½ yards of 1½"-wide green
   plaid ribbon
9 yards of ⅝"-wide green
   double-faced satin ribbon
Straight pins
Iron and press cloth
Matching sewing thread
3 yards of narrow sew-in red piping
½ yard of 45"-wide red cotton fabric
2—5½"-long red tassels
2—5½"-long green tassels

INSTRUCTIONS

To make the table runner shape, use the fabric marking pencil to draw a 15½×39" rectangle centered on the nonfusible side of the interfacing. Referring to the diagram *opposite,* mark the center of the short edge of the rectangle, measuring 7¾" in from a long edge of the rectangle. From the short edge of the rectangle, measure 6¾" up on each long edge; mark. Draw a line connecting each side mark to the center mark, making a large V. Repeat for the other short edge. Do not cut out; these are the sewing lines.

Cut the ribbons as follows: seven 41" lengths of red plaid; eight 41" lengths of red velvet; 19—18" lengths of green plaid; and 18—18" lengths of green satin.

Place the interfacing fusible side up on a flat ironing surface. Beginning at the center of the table runner shape with a plaid ribbon, place the 41" ribbon lengths side by side on the interfacing, alternating the ribbons.

Position the ribbons over the shape so an even amount of ribbon extends beyond the edges of the points. Pin the ribbon ends to the interfacing.

Beginning at the center of the table runner shape with a plaid ribbon, weave the 18" ribbon lengths over and under the long ribbons. Alternate the ribbons and position on the shape with an even amount of ribbon extending beyond the long edges. Pin the ribbon ends to the interfacing.

Use an iron and press cloth to fuse the woven ribbons to the interfacing, following the manufacturer's instructions. Remove the pins. Press on the interfacing side. With the interfacing side up, baste on the drawn lines that indicate the table runner shape. For the table runner front,

trim the fused ribbons/interfacing ⅜" beyond the basting stitches. Using the table runner front as a pattern, cut one matching shape from the red cotton fabric for the back.

Use a zipper foot to sew the piping to the front of the table runner with the sewing line of the piping atop the basting stitches on the table runner front, overlapping the ends on one long edge. With right sides together, sew the table runner front and back together, leaving an opening on one long edge for turning. Trim the seams, clip the corners, and turn right side out. Press. Slip-stitch the opening closed. Sew tassels to the back at the points.

—*Designed by Margaret Sindelar*

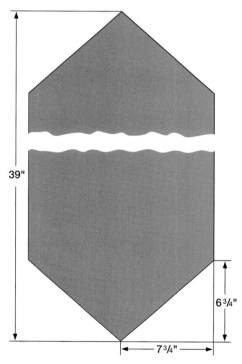

Plaid-Trimmed Tree Skirt

Shown below and opposite.

YOU WILL NEED
1¼ yard of 45"-wide red corduroy
1¼ yard of 45"-wide green velveteen
1¼ yard each of 45"-wide red and
    green cotton fabric for backs
Fabric marking pencil
Yardstick
5 yards of 1½"-wide red
    plaid ribbon
5 yards of 1½"-wide green
    plaid ribbon
3 yards of ⅞"-wide red plaid ribbon
Matching sewing thread
4—5½"-long red tassels
4—5½"-long green tassels
3—1⅞"-diameter button cover forms

INSTRUCTIONS

Cut a 41" square from both the red corduroy and the green velveteen fabrics for the skirt fronts.

From both the red and the green cotton fabrics, cut a 41" square for the skirt backs. To find the center, fold the red skirt back into quarters, creating a smaller square. Lightly press the folds to serve as placement guides; unfold and smooth out the fabric, wrong side up, on a flat surface. For the tree trunk opening, draw a 4"-diameter circle on the skirt back, centering the circle on the fabric where the creases intersect. For the center back opening, use a yardstick to draw a line from the center to the outer edge along one of the creases. For the green skirt back, fold the fabric into quarters diagonally, creating a triangle. Continue as for the red back.

With right sides facing, pin the red skirt front and back together along the edges and drawn lines. Using a ½" seam allowance, sew the outer edges of the red front and back together, leaving a 6" opening on one edge for turning; continue sewing ¼" from the circle and on both sides of the center back line. Carefully cut on the drawn line and trim the seam allowance of the circle to ¼". Trim the seams, and clip the curves. Turn the skirt right side out; sew the opening closed. Press.

Pin the green plaid ribbon along the outer edges of the red tree skirt, mitering the ribbon at the corners and turning under the raw ends at the center back. Sew the ribbon to the skirt along the long edges.

Repeat for the green skirt front and back and 1½"-wide red plaid ribbon.

With right sides up, layer the red skirt on top of the green skirt, aligning the edges of the tree trunk openings and the left and right edges of the center backs. The green skirt will extend beyond the red skirt at the center back. Topstitch the skirts together ¼" from the center back and trunk opening edges.

For the ties, cut the ⅞"-wide red plaid ribbon into six 18" lengths. Sew the ribbons in pairs along the left and right center back edges, positioning them at the top, bottom, and center of the red skirt.

Cover the three button forms with green velveteen fabric, following the manufacturer's instructions. Sewing through all fabric layers, center the buttons on the front and side edges of the red skirt, 3½" in from the plaid ribbon. Sew a red tassel to each of the four corners of the red skirt and a green tassel to each of the four corners of the green skirt.

—Designed by Margaret Sindelar

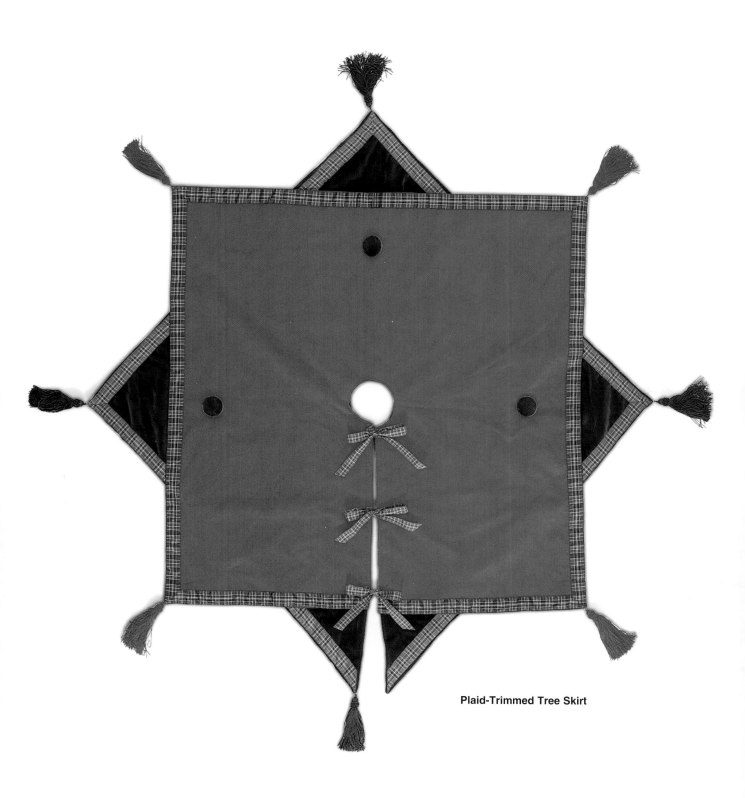

Plaid-Trimmed Tree Skirt

Woven Ribbon Cone Ornament

Shown below.

YOU WILL NEED

For each ornament:

10" square of fusible nonwoven firm interfacing

Fabric marking pencil

Tracing paper

3¾ yards of ⅝"-wide red velvet ribbon

3¾ yards of ⅝"-wide forest double-faced satin ribbon

Straight pins

Iron and press cloth

Matching sewing thread

12" length of fabric-covered wire

¾ yard of 1½"-wide red plaid ribbon

INSTRUCTIONS

Use the fabric marking pencil to draw an 8" square centered on the nonfusible side of the interfacing. Trace the cone pattern *opposite* onto the tracing paper; cut out the pattern. Position the cone pattern on the nonfusible side of the interfacing with the straight edges of the pattern aligned with two adjacent lines of the square. Trace the cone shape onto the interfacing.

Cut thirteen 10" lengths of red velvet ribbon and thirteen 10" lengths of forest satin ribbon.

Place the interfacing fusible side up on a flat ironing surface. Place the red ribbon lengths side by side on the interfacing with an even amount of ribbon extending beyond the top and bottom edges of the square. Pin the ribbon ends to the interfacing.

Weave the forest ribbon lengths over and under the red ribbons with an even amount of ribbon extending beyond the left and right edges. Pin the ribbon ends to the interfacing.

Use an iron and press cloth to fuse the woven ribbons to the interfacing, following the manufacturer's instructions. Remove the pins. Press on the interfacing side. With the interfacing side up, baste on the drawn lines that indicate the cone shape. Trim the fused ribbons/interfacing ⅜" beyond the basting stitches on the straight edges and a scant ⅛" beyond the basting stitches on the curved edge.

To bind the curved edge, fold the remaining red velvet ribbon over the raw edge; edge-stitch in place. With right sides together, sew together the straight edges of the cone using a ¼" seam allowance. Turn the cone right side out.

For the handle, fold the 1½"-wide plaid ribbon in half lengthwise; sew ⅛" from the edge, forming a tube. Turn the tube right side out. Slip the fabric-covered wire into the tube. Make a knot in the ribbon tube at each end of the wire. With the ends of the tube and the wire even, sew the handle to opposite sides of the cone above the knots.

—Designed by Margaret Sindelar

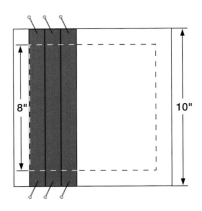

8"   10"

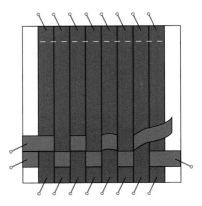

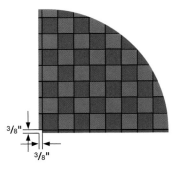

⅜"

⅜"

Woven Ribbon Cone Ornament
Cut 1

Embossed Velvet Boxes

Shown on page 38 and below.

YOU WILL NEED

Rayon/acetate velvet: ¾ yard of green for the large box and ⅜ yard of ivory for the small box

6" and 8" square papier-mâché square boxes

Delta Ceramcoat Acrylic Paint: Light Ivory #2401 and Silver Pine #2534

Paintbrush; small sea sponge

Delta Pearl Luster Medium

12×12" sheet of cork (⁵⁄₃₂" thick)

Self-healing cutting mat

Crafts knife

V-shape gouge

Steam iron and press cloth

Spray bottle for water

Dark graphite paper

2½×6" floral lace spray appliqués

1×15" piece of scalloped lace

Water erasable marking pen

Tracing paper

26" of ⅜"-deep white lace heart trim

⅔ yard of ivory rayon braid

2 yards of green rayon braid

4 green tassels

Frosted-white glass "E" beads

Pearl glass seed beads

Hand-sewing needle

Ivory and green sewing threads

Permanent fabric adhesive

INSTRUCTIONS

Finish the insides of the boxes and lids first. Base-coat the insides of both boxes and both lids with Light Ivory acrylic paint. Let dry. Sponge paint the inside of the large box and lid using the sea sponge and Silver Pine. Allow to dry.

For the large box, mix one part Silver Pine with one part Pearl Luster Medium. Repeat the sponge-painting process over the sponged layer. For the ivory box, mix Light Ivory with the Pearl Luster Medium; sponge the mixture over the base coat. Allow the paint to dry.

TO MAKE CORK TEMPLATE

To make the cork template for the white box, place two floral lace sprays on the sheet of cork. Trace around the lace shapes with the water-erasable marking pencil. Remove the lace shapes from the cork. Place the cork on a self-healing mat and cut out the traced shape using the crafts knife. Set the lace and cork aside.

To make the cork template for the green box, trace the fleur-de-lis pattern and transfer the traced lines to the cork using the graphite paper. Cut out the cork shape on the outside lines as before. Use the V-shape gouge to cut ¹⁄₁₆"-deep grooves on one side of the cork for the inside design lines of the fleur-de-lis.

CUTTING THE FABRIC

For the ivory box and lid, cut the following pieces of ivory velvet:

- 1—20×6¼" piece for two sides/bottom of the box
- 2—7¼×6¼" pieces for the opposite sides of the box
- 1—9×6½ piece for the top and two sides of the lid
- 2—6½×1¾" pieces for the opposite sides of the lid

For the green box and lid, cut the following pieces of green velvet:

- 1—26×8½" piece for two sides/bottom of the box
- 2—9½×9" pieces for the opposite sides of the box
- 1—11¾×8½" piece for the top and two sides of the lid
- 2—2¼×9" pieces for the opposite sides of the lid

EMBOSSING THE VELVET

To emboss the ivory velvet for the small box, fill the iron with water; preheat the iron to medium setting. Fold a bath towel in half and place it on a hard work surface. Place the 20×6¼" piece of velvet right side up, on the towel. Lay the floral lace spray appliqués 2" from the top and approximately 1" from the edges.

Spray the lace and velvet lightly with water. Cover the lace appliqués with the matching cork template. Cover the cork with a press cloth. Dampen a hand towel with water, wringing out most of the water. Place the dampened towel over the press cloth. Place the iron over the dampened towel and press down with a steady, firm pressure for 15 seconds. Remove the towel, press cloth, cork, and lace appliqués to check the impressions. If more embossing is needed, replace the lace, cork, press cloth, and towel; press for an additional 10 seconds.

Remove the towel, press cloth, templates, and lace. Repeat the embossing process on the other end of ivory velvet. Place a 7¼×6¼" piece of velvet, right side up, on the bath towel. Repeat the embossing process, placing the lace appliqués 2" from the top and 1" from sides. Repeat for the remaining 7¼×6¼" piece of velvet.

For the lid, place the 9×6½" piece of ivory velvet, right side up, on the towel. Center the appliqués 1¼" from the top and bottom and ¾" from sides. Cover with the cork templates. Cut two 6½" lengths from the scalloped lace. Place these lengths horizontally across the velvet lid sides, ¾" from the top and bottom edges. No cork templates are needed. Repeat the embossing process. Place the 6½×13¾" pieces of velvet, right sides up, on the bath towel. Place the 6½" lengths of lace, ¾" from the bottom edges of velvet. Emboss as above. Allow all velvet pieces to dry.

Thread a needle with ivory thread to randomly hand-sew pearl seed beads and frosted white glass "E" beads to the floral impressions. Set aside the ivory velvet pieces.

For the green velvet box, place the 26×8½" piece of green velvet right side up on the bath towel. Place the fleur-de-lis cork template on the velvet, centered, 2½" from the top and 1½" from the sides. The gouged lines face the velvet. To avoid a textured background on the velvet, do not use a press cloth. Place a damp towel directly over the cork template and emboss as for the ivory box. Repeat the embossing process at the opposite end of the velvet. Emboss both 9½×9" pieces for the box sides and the center of the 11¾×8½" piece for the lid.

COVERING THE BOXES
To cover each box, use the permanent fabric adhesive to adhere the opposite two sides of velvet to the appropriate box. Turn under approximately ⅜" hems on both long edges of the two sides/bottom piece. Use adhesive to attach the piece to the box, covering all raw velvet edges.

Embossed Velvet Box
Fleur-de-lis Pattern

Wrap and glue the top edges of velvet over the top edges of the box. Glue the coordinating rayon braid around the inside of each box, covering the raw edges of the velvet; trim off excess braid. Cover the lids in the same manner, except position the velvet pieces next to the bottom edges of the box lid.

Glue the white lace heart trim around the bottom edge of the ivory box lid; trim excess lace. Glue the remaining green rayon braid around the bottom edge of the green lid; trim off excess braid. Using green thread, stitch the green tassels to the bottom corners of the lid.
—*Designed by Brenda Spitzer*

The Angels Sing

Have an angelic holiday! The presence of angels makes your holiday decor simply celestial. Decorate a fragrant fresh-cut holiday tree with handmade ornaments inspired by cloud-hopping, music-playing winged creatures: musical notes topped with feathers, flower-filled whitewashed tins, lace teardrops, lilac nosegays, and miniature French-style chairs (below) with lute-playing angels stamped on the silk cushions. Instructions begin on page 48.

A rustic cherub (opposite) creates a divine table centerpiece or sideboard decor. Combine unfinished wood turnings, papier-mâché, and paint—and behold the delightful transformation to shabby-chic angel. Harps that serve appropriately as wings are ornamented with delicate teardrop prisms to catch heavenly rays of holiday light.

White silk dupioni stockings (left) are as soft as clouds—and a becoming surface for angels to light. Trace the illustrations onto the stocking fronts to handpaint this musical duo. Back the stockings with black velvet, top them with fused ribbon, and fill them to the brim to prop or hang from the mantel.

Salt Shaker Angel Ornament

Shown on page 45 and right.

YOU WILL NEED

**Vintage clear glass shaker,
    measuring about 2¾" tall**
Several shades of glass paint
Glitter
Plastic cup
**24" length of 16-gauge
    silver-plated wire**
Wire cutters
Hammer
Needle-nose pliers
**18" length of 24-gauge
    silver-plated wire**
Vintage bauble for head
Industrial adhesive

French Chair Ornament

Shown on page 44.

YOU WILL NEED

Tracing paper
¼ yard of ivory silk dupioni
**6×12" piece of white
    crescent cardboard**
Crafts knife
Crafts glue
4⅝×1⅜" woodturnings for legs
**2¼×1⅝" wooden spindles for
    chair back**
**Acrylic paint: ivory and
    gold metallic**
Paintbrush
Sealer
Masking tape
4 clothespins
Angel rubber stamp, about 2" tall
Black fabric ink pad
Batting scraps
¼ yard of narrow black trim
½ yard of 7mm green silk ribbon
**Glue gun and hotmelt
    adhesive sticks**
4" length of 4mm green silk ribbon
½ yard of 1"-wide green ribbon
Black gel pen
Ruler
Foam brush
Iron

INSTRUCTIONS

Search local antiques stores for crystal or glass salt and pepper shakers. Wash and dry the shaker.

Pour several shades of glass paint into the shaker and swirl the paint to completely cover the inside of the shaker. (For a glittered angel, pour glitter into the shaker before adding the paint.) Place the shaker upside down in a paper cup so the shaker rests in the cup without touching

the bottom. Let the paint drip and dry completely.

To form the wings and halo, use a 24" length of 16-gauge silver-plated wire and refer to the illustrations *below left*. Bend one end of the wire into a wing shape, measuring about 3½"-long, for the left wing. Twist the wire around itself about 1" from the tip of the wing. Shape the right wing in the same manner and wrap the wire around itself between the wings for the center back. Bend the wire up and make a 1"-diameter circle for the halo. Bring the wire down and wrap around the center back of wings. Trim any excess wire with the wire cutter and flatten the end with a hammer.

To attach the wings and halo to the shaker, cut an 18" length of 24-gauge wire. Place the center of the wire on the center front neck of the shaker. Wrap the wire twice around the neck. Place the center back of the wings against the shaker at the back of the neck and wrap the wire snugly around the wings to secure. Trim the wire ends and tuck them under. For the head, use industrial adhesive to glue the bauble to the top of the shaker.

—Designed by Mary Jo Hiney

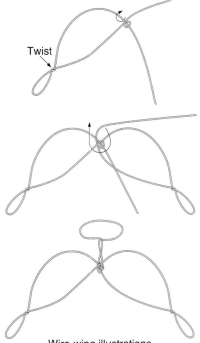

Twist

Wire-wing illustrations

INSTRUCTIONS

Trace the three chair patterns *opposite* onto tracing paper. Cut out each pattern piece.

Trace the stabilizer and seat once and the back twice on the silk dupioni. Cut out the fabric pieces ¾" beyond the drawn lines. Trace the seat and back twice, and the stabilizer once on the cardboard. Cut out the cardboard pieces on the drawn lines and use the crafts knife to score the cardboard stabilizer piece as indicated by the dashed line on the pattern. Glue one seat to the unscored side of the stabilizer.

Apply a thin coat of crafts glue to the scored side of the cardboard stabilizer. Center and smooth the

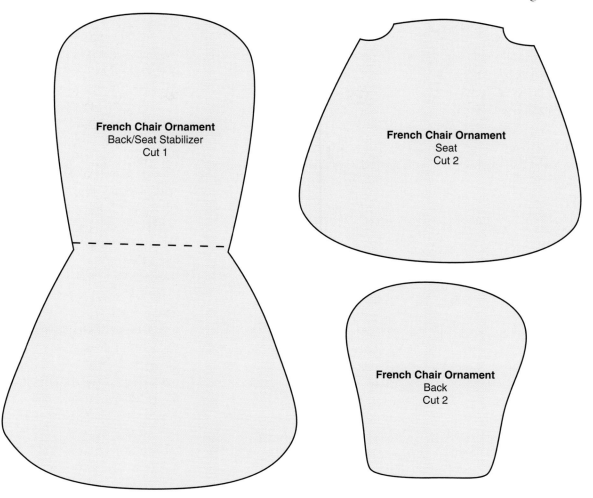

French Chair Ornament
Back/Seat Stabilizer
Cut 1

French Chair Ornament
Seat
Cut 2

French Chair Ornament
Back
Cut 2

stabilizer fabric, wrong side down, over the glued side of the cardboard piece. Carefully fold and glue the raw edges of the fabric around the cardboard shape, clipping and trimming as necessary. Press the stabilizer firmly against a flat surface to flatten; fold on the score line.

Base-coat the woodturnings and spindles ivory; let dry. Apply a thin coat of gold metallic paint to all ivory surfaces; let dry. Then apply a coat of sealer. Let the sealer dry.

To make the chair, bend the stabilizer in position along the score line and use masking tape to hold the chair in place. Use crafts glue to glue the spindles to the left and right edges of the chair back with the bottom of the spindles on the seat. Use clothespins to hold the spindles in place, wiping away excess glue. Let the glue dry thoroughly.

Ink the angel stamp with black and apply it to the center of one chair back fabric piece. Use the gel pen to add detail to the stamped image and to write a Christmas message centered on the seat fabric. Heat-set both fabric pieces with an iron.

Glue a batting scrap to one side of each of the cardboard backs and to the remaining cardboard seat. Trim the batting even with the edges of the cardboard pieces. To cover the cardboard pieces with fabric, place the corresponding fabric piece wrong side down on the batting side of the cardboard piece. Fold the raw edges of the fabric around the cardboard shape and glue in place, clipping and trimming as necessary.

Hot-glue the 7mm green silk ribbon to the wrong side of the padded seat, making even folded loops that extend about ⅛" beyond

the edges of the seat. Hot-glue the black trim to the wrong side of one padded back, letting the trim extend about 1⁄16" beyond the edges of the back. For the hanging loop, fold the 4" length of 4mm green silk ribbon in half. Hot-glue the ends to the top center on the wrong side of the second padded back. Center and glue the 1"-wide green ribbon across the wrong side of the padded back with the bottom edges even.

Hot-glue the padded seat to the top of the chair seat, aligning the curves at the back of the padded seat with the spindles. Glue the padded backs to the chair back. For the legs, glue the woodturnings to the corners on the bottom of the chair seat. Tie the 1"-wide ribbon into a bow at the back of the chair.
—*Designed by Mary Jo Hiney*

Tin Washbasin Ornament

Shown on page 45 and below right.

YOU WILL NEED
5½×4×1¾" tin washbasin
Ivory acrylic paint
1" foam brush
Dove rubber stamp
Black pigment ink pad
Clear embossing powder
Embossing heat tool
Spray sealer
Florist's foam
Glue gun and hotmelt
     adhesive sticks
Moss or excelsior
5 sprays of velvet and satin leaves
     in shades of green
Spray each of ivory vintage freesia,
     vintage fern, and berries
Wire cutters
1¼ yards of ½"-wide light green
     grosgrain ribbon

INSTRUCTIONS

Use the foam brush to paint the washbasin with two coats of ivory, letting dry between coats. Ink the dove stamp with black ink and stamp the image three times along the front and back bottom edges of the basin, re-inking the stamp after each impression. Sprinkle the wet ink immediately with clear embossing powder. Tap off the excess powder. Use the embossing tool to melt the powder, creating a shiny, raised image. Apply two light coats of spray sealer to the basin, letting the sealer dry between coats.

To fill the bottom of the basin, cut a thin slice of florist's foam and hot-glue it to the inside bottom of the basin. Cover the foam with moss or excelsior; glue in place. Cut the leaf sprays, and glue the sprays to the moss around the edge of the basin. Cut, arrange, and glue the berry, freesia, and fern sprays inside the basin. Fill in open areas with extra dried materials or leaves.

For the hanging loop, slip the ribbon through the basin handles. Knot the ribbon ends around the center of the ribbon, leaving long tails for a bow. Tie the ribbon ends into a bow.
—*Designed by Mary Jo Hiney*

Musical Note Ornament

Shown on page 45 and below.

YOU WILL NEED
5½" length of ¼"-diameter
     wooden dowel
2½"-diameter foam ball
Acrylic paint: apple green and
     gold metallic
Paintbrush
44"-long white goose feathers
23"-long white marabou feathers
24" length of 26-gauge black wire
Wire cutters
Crafts glue
Velvet leaves: 4 green and
     9 pale green
Satin leaves: 12 pale green
Tiny holeless clear glass beads
Gold glitter

INSTRUCTIONS

Use the dowel to make a deep hole in the foam ball close to one side; remove the dowel. Paint the dowel apple green and the goose feathers with a sheer coat of gold metallic. Let the paint dry.

Form a hanging loop at the center of the 26-gauge black wire. Position the loop at the top of the painted dowel and diagonally wrap the remaining wire to crisscross around the dowel. Securely twist the wire about 1" from the bottom of the dowel; trim off the excess wire with wire cutters. Squeeze glue into the hole in the ball, insert the dowel, and let the glue dry.

Set aside five satin leaves. Beginning at the bottom, randomly cover the ball with the remaining leaves, overlapping the leaves to cover the ball completely. To attach the leaves, coat the back of each leaf with glue and press onto the ball.

To attach the beads, apply glue irregularly to the top of the ball, letting it run down onto the sides. Immediately pour the clear holeless beads onto the glue. Press the beads into the glue; shake off the excess. While the glue is wet, sprinkle with gold glitter. Let the glue dry.

Glue three satin leaves to the ball around the base of the dowel. Glue the goose feathers to the front top of the dowel and the marabou feathers to the back of the goose feathers. Use a satin leaf to cover the ends of the marabou feathers, wrapping the wide end of the leaf around the dowel to the front. Glue the remaining satin leaf to the front of the goose feathers, covering the quill ends and wrapping the wide end of the leaf to the back.

Lightly dab glue onto the three leaves at the base of the dowel and onto the dowel. Pour the clear holeless beads onto the glue and sprinkle with glitter. Let the glue dry.
—*Designed by Mary Jo Hiney*

Lace Teardrop Ornament

Shown on page 45 and right.

YOU WILL NEED

2—2½×4" glass teardrop shapes

Fabric glue

Scrap of ivory lace, measuring about 3×4½"

Crafts glue

Foam brush

12" length of 4mm-wide ivory silk ribbon and ⅜"-wide ivory gimp trim

Window cleaner and paper towels

24" length of 1"-wide ivory bias-cut silk ribbon

Large-eye needle

INSTRUCTIONS

Wash and dry the glass teardrop shapes. Use the foam brush to spread a thin layer of fabric glue onto one side of one glass teardrop. Smooth the vintage lace, right side up, onto the glue. Trim the lace a scant ⅛" beyond the edges of the glass teardrop. Spread crafts glue onto the edge of the teardrop and smooth the edges of the lace onto the glue. Wipe off any excess glue from the back of the teardrop.

Place the second glass teardrop over the lace. Thread the 4mm-wide silk ribbon through the holes at the top of the teardrops and tie into a knot. Trim the ribbon ends ½" beyond the knot and glue the ends to the edges of the teardrops.

Spread crafts glue onto the edges of the teardrops. Wrap the remaining ¼"-wide silk ribbon around the teardrop, smoothing it onto the glue. Spread crafts glue onto the wrong side of the gimp trim. Beginning at the top of the teardrop, smooth the gimp trim around the edges of the teardrop. Trim the gimp cord even at the top of the teardrop. Dab extra glue on the cut ends of the gimp cord to prevent raveling.

Spray window cleaner onto a paper towel and clean the front and back of the ornament. For the hanging loop, thread the 1"-wide bias-cut silk ribbon into the large-eye needle and then through the hole at the top of the ornament. Tie a bow near the ends of the ribbon.
—*Designed by Mary Jo Hiney*

Paris Clock Ornament

Shown on page 45 and above.

YOU WILL NEED

3½×3¾" wooden dollhouse window frame with a 1¾×2⅛" windowpane opening

Acrylic paint: gold metallic and two shades of ivory

Paintbrush and sponge

8½×11" sheet of ivory paper

Photo copier

13" length of ⅛"-wide ivory satin ribbon

Crafts glue

Scrap of poster board

INSTRUCTIONS

Remove the windowpane from the window frame. Paint the wooden frame ivory, using the shades

randomly. Apply a second coat, letting the paint dry between coats. Dab gold metallic paint onto the frame to highlight.

Photo copy the clock face *below* onto the ivory paper. Trim the clock face and the poster board to fit in the windowpane opening. To age the clock face, lightly sponge with ivory paint; let the paint dry. Insert the clock face and the poster board in the opening; glue in place.

For the hanging loop, glue the ribbon around the edges of the frame with the ribbon loop at the top edge.
—*Designed by Mary Jo Hiney*

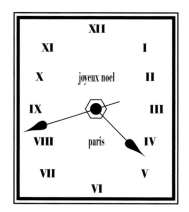

Clockface pattern

Tabletop Angel

Shown on page 46.

YOU WILL NEED

2 woodturnings, one each
measuring about 4½×9¼"
and 3¾×5½"
Wood glue
Hammer and nails; drill
2 wood shapes for wings
Celluclay instant papier-mâché
Waxed paper
Dust mask
Resealable plastic bag
Aluminum foil
Crafts glue
Spackle
Gesso
Paintbrush and foam brush
Weathered rust paint
Crackle medium
Acrylic paint: several shades of
ivory and dusty rose
Water-base satin finish
2 chandelier crystals,
about 2½"-long
Fine-gauge copper wire

INSTRUCTIONS

Use wood glue to glue the bottom of the small wood turning to the top of the large wood turning. Nail the turnings together; sink the nails. Drill small holes in the wood wing shapes to hang the crystals. To attach the wings, drill holes in the base of the shapes to accommodate nails. Nail the wings to opposite sides of the small wood turning.

Line the work area with waxed paper. For safety, wear a dust mask to avoid breathing papier-mâché dust. Mix a quarter of the package of the instant papier-mâché with water, following the manufacturer's instructions. Keep unused papier-mâché mixture in a resealable plastic bag while you work, and refrigerate the mixture in the bag for future use.

For the head, crumple a piece of aluminum foil into a 2- to 2½"-diameter ball around the top of the small woodturning. Moisten your fingers with water and apply a thin, even coat of the papier-mâché mixture to the ball. Allow the mixture to dry. Glue the head to the wood turning. Add more of the papier-mâché mixture to build up the head. Pinch the mixture between your fingers for the nose at the center of the face. Use your fingertips to slightly indent oval areas for the eyes and mouth. Let the head dry completely. Drill a tiny hole in the back of the head for the halo.

Spackle and fill the nail holes. To create texture, use the paintbrush to apply a haphazard coat of gesso on the wood turnings. Apply a light coat of gesso to the wings and head. Let the gesso dry completely.

Paint all surfaces of the angel with the weathered rust paint. When the paint is completely dry, apply an even layer of crackle medium and let dry, following the manufacturer's instructions. Paint all crackle medium surfaces ivory, using the shades randomly. When the paint is dry, apply a coat of satin finish to all surfaces.

Use wire to attach the chandelier crystals to the predrilled holes in the wings. For the halo, shape the copper wire into a circle about 2¼" in diameter, wrapping the wire around about four times. Wrap the circles of wire together by twisting the wire around the circle. To attach the halo, cut an 8" length of wire. Secure the wire to the halo with the center of the wire at the center back of the halo and twist together the wire ends. Trim the wire

to the desired length and glue the ends in the predrilled hole at the back of the head. Lightly blush the angel's cheeks with dusty rose paint.
—*Designed by Mary Jo Hiney*

Gilded Lilac Bouquet

Shown on pages 45–46 and below.

YOU WILL NEED

Purchased reproduction lilac
spray
Foam brush
Glitter glue
Gold glitter

INSTRUCTIONS

Using the foam brush, lightly and randomly touch the tips of the leaves and the flowers with the glitter glue. Lightly sprinkle the gold glitter over the glue. Shake off the excess glitter and let the glue dry.
—*Designed by Mary Jo Hiney*

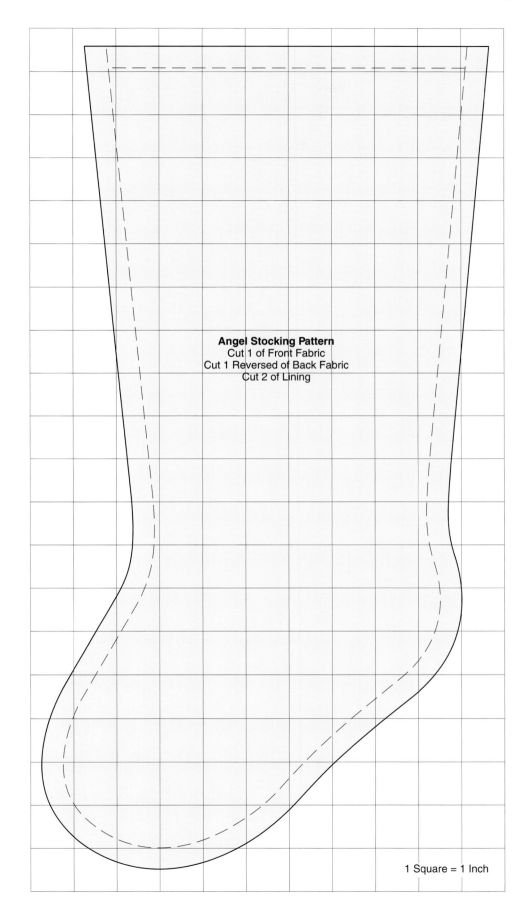

Angel Stocking Pattern
Cut 1 of Front Fabric
Cut 1 Reversed of Back Fabric
Cut 2 of Lining

1 Square = 1 Inch

INSTRUCTIONS

Trace one section of the angel pattern, *above right,* onto tracing paper. Reposition the tracing paper over the remaining angel section, *opposite,* matching the design lines; complete the tracing. Enlarge the stocking pattern, *page 53,* on graph paper. Cut out the pattern piece. Sew all pieces with right sides together using ½" seam allowances, unless otherwise noted.

CUT THE FABRICS

Use the stocking pattern to cut one stocking front and two lining pieces from the ivory silk dupioni fabric. From the black velvet fabric, reverse the pattern, and cut one stocking back. If desired, cut 2×10" strips of black velvet for trim at the top of the stocking.

PAINT THE ANGEL

Tape the angel tracing onto a strong light source, such as a light box. Position and tape the stocking front, right side up, over the angel tracing.

Use the #0 liner brush and black to paint the finer lines of the design. Draw the brush freely, letting the paint feather out. Use the #2 liner brush to paint the remaining design lines. Let the paint dry. Use an iron to heat-set the paint, following the manufacturer's instructions.

SEW THE STOCKING

To add ribbon and gimp trim to the stocking front, pin the 1½"-wide ribbon across the stocking ⅝" from the top edge; sew the raw edges in place. Position the gimp on the ribbon ⅛" below the top edge of the ribbon. Use black thread to zigzag-stitch along the center of the gimp.

To add velvet and ribbon trim to the stocking front, position the 2×10" velvet strip, right side down, across the stocking ½" below the top edge. Sew the velvet strip to the stocking, sewing ½" from the top edge of the strip. Fold the velvet strip up, trim the edges even with the sides of the stocking, and baste the side and top edges in place. From the 1"-wide ribbon, cut a 15" and 9" length. Pin one end of each ribbon length to the sides of the stocking, 1" below the top edge of the stocking. Position the long length on the toe edge and the short length on the heel edge.

Sew the stocking front to the back, leaving the top edge open. To prevent the velvet from moving, place a sheet of tissue paper underneath the velvet when sewing. Trim the seam

allowances, and clip the curves. Turn the stocking right side out.

Sew the stocking lining pieces together, leaving the top edge open and a 4" opening on one side for turning. Trim the seam allowances, and clip the curves; do not turn the lining right side out. Slip the stocking inside the lining with right sides together. Sew the stocking to the lining at the top edges. Turn the stocking and lining right side out through the side opening. Slip-stitch the opening closed. Tuck the lining into the stocking.

For the hanging loop, fold a 5" length of black gimp trim in half. Sew the ends to the top inside corner on the heel side of the stocking.
—*Designed by Mary Jo Hiney*

A Fine & Fancy
Holiday Ensemble

Dress any room for the holidays with understated holiday hues of sage, cream, and rose (opposite). Curl up comfortably beside a blazing fireplace that has handmade stockings hung to the side. Wrap yourself in a damask throw, that coordinates with the stockings, for added warmth. Sit back to relish the heartfelt holiday mantel message of "Love," "Peace," and "Joy." Fresh-cut arrangements of roses and greenery add fragrance and beauty to the holiday setting. Instructions begin on page 62.

Slipcover your mantel with warm sentiments of the season. Cream-color damask pennants (opposite) declare "Love," "Peace," and "Joy," and alternate with dark sage button-trimmed velvet for a holiday harlequin look.

Mix seasonal greens with cream-color roses for a fresh twist on a traditional holiday centerpiece. Sprigs of fragrant rosemary and blue-green eucalyptus are interspersed with rose-color pepperberries to frame buttery florist roses. Top the arrangement with a gilded bow for a centerpiece that is fragrant and fancy!

titch a striped damask and velvet throw, then cuddle up in cushy comfort in front of a roaring fire. Our easy-to-assemble throw is filled with quilt batting for cozy warmth. Decorated in one corner with a fabric flower and edged with luxurious fringe, the candy-cane stripe throw is as decorative tossed over the back of a chair as it is cozy to snuggle under.

Hang these stockings by the chimney with care (to have Santa fill them with sweet treats). Made from embossed velvet and damask, our holiday stockings kick up a little fun wherever they hang out.

Love, Peace, and Joy Mantel Cloth

Shown on pages 57–58.

The finished mantel cloth is 73" long.

YOU WILL NEED

Graph paper

¾ yard of 54"-wide ivory brocade fabric

2⅛ yards of green embossed velvet

½ yard of rose-stripe fabric

2⅛ yards of muslin for lining

⅛ yard of gold metallic fabric for buttons

Matching sewing threads; gold metallic thread

1 yard of cotton batting

2¼ yards of ¼"-diameter gold metallic sew-in twisted cording

6—2"-diameter self-cover button forms

INSTRUCTIONS

Enlarge the top and bottom triangle patterns, *opposite,* on graph paper. Add ½" seam allowances beyond the drawn lines and cut out the completed pattern pieces. Sew all pieces with right sides together, using ½" seam allowances, unless otherwise noted.

EMBROIDER THE FABRIC

From the ivory brocade fabric, cut three 18×27" rectangles. Take the fabric rectangles to a custom embroidery shop to have them embroider "Love," "Peace," and "Joy" on the rectangles with gold metallic thread. Each word should be centered on a rectangle with the bottom of the lettering 10" from the top edge of the fabric.

CUT THE FABRICS

From the embroidered ivory brocade fabric rectangles, cut:

- 3 top triangles, positioning the words as indicated in the triangle before cutting

From the green embossed velvet, cut:

- 1—7×74" strip and 6 bottom triangles

From the rose-stripe fabric, cut:

- 2 top triangles

From the muslin, cut:

- 1—7×74" strip, 6 bottom triangles, and 5 top triangles

From the cotton batting, cut:

- 5 top triangles

SEW THE MANTEL SCARF

To assemble the top triangles, place the embroidered brocade triangles and rose-stripe triangles right side down on matching muslin triangles. Layer a batting triangle on the wrong side of the embroidered brocade triangles and rose-stripe triangles. Sew together all layers on the long edges of the triangles, leaving the top edge open. Trim the seam allowances, turn right side out, and press. Machine-baste the raw edges together.

To assemble the bottom triangles, place the green embossed velvet triangles right side down on a matching muslin triangle. Sew the triangles together on the long edges, leaving the top edge open. Trim the seam allowances, turn right side out, and press. Machine-baste the raw edges together.

Smooth the 7×74" muslin strip on a flat surface; the side of the strip facing up will be the right side of the strip. Position the bottom triangles, right side up, on the muslin strip with the raw edges of the triangles aligned with the top long edge of the strip. Space the bottom triangles about ½" apart and at least ½" from the short edges of the strip; baste the triangles to the strip.

Referring to the diagram, *below,* position the rose-stripe top triangles and embroidered brocade top triangles on the strip with the raw edges even, centering the top triangles between the bottom triangles. The triangles should be about 2¼" apart. Baste the top triangles in place. Press the muslin strip away from the triangles.

Using a zipper foot, sew the gold metallic cording to one long edge of the 7×74" green embossed velvet strip. Press under the cording seam allowance for the bottom edge of the velvet strip. With right sides together, pin the velvet strip to the muslin strip. Sew the strips together along the short and top edges. Trim the seam allowances, clip the corners, and turn the strip right side out. Carefully press the velvet strip to cover the seam allowances and basting stitches of the triangles. Sew the cording edge of the strip in place, using a zipper foot to sew as close to the cording as possible.

FINISH THE MANTEL SCARF

Use gold metallic thread to machine-quilt a square grid on the long velvet strip at the top of the mantel scarf, sewing diagonal lines 3" apart.

Cover six button forms with gold metallic fabric, following the button manufacturer's instructions. Sew a button to each bottom triangle, centered on the triangle about 5" above the point.

—Designed by Lenny Houts

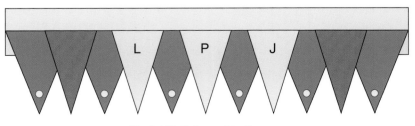

Mantel Cloth Assembly diagram

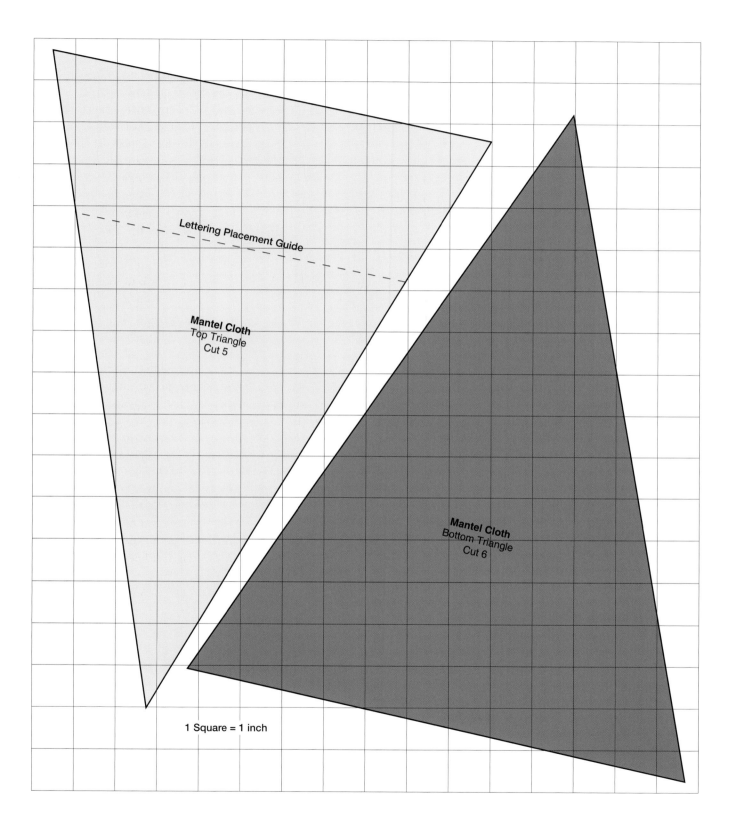

Lettering Placement Guide

Mantel Cloth
Top Triangle
Cut 5

Mantel Cloth
Bottom Triangle
Cut 6

1 Square = 1 inch

Elegant Striped Lap Quilt

Shown on page 57 and 61.

The finished lap quilt is 46×63", excluding the fringe.

YOU WILL NEED

Tracing paper

1¾ yards of green embossed velvet

1¾ yards of ivory velvet

3½ yards of 54"-wide ivory brocade for strips and backing

2 yards of rose-stripe fabric

48×65" piece of cotton batting

Matching sewing threads

Gold metallic thread

6 yards of 6"-wide boucle fringe

Scrap of non-woven sew-in interfacing

Scrap of gold metallic fabric for button

2"-diameter self-cover button form

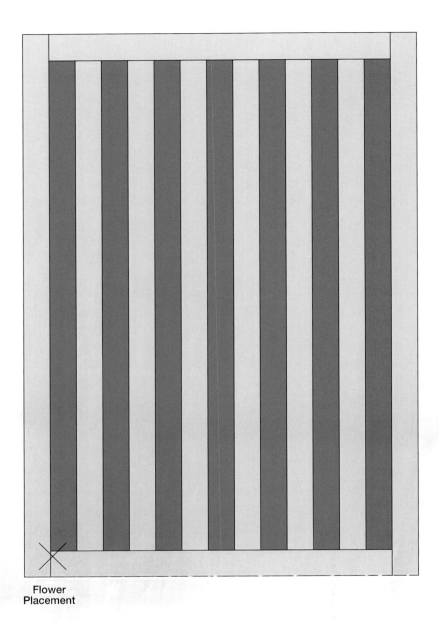

Flower
Placement

INSTRUCTIONS

Trace the flower petal/leaf pattern *opposite* onto tracing paper; add ½" seam allowances beyond the drawn line and cut out the pattern piece. The fabric quantities specified in the materials list are for 44/45"-wide fabric unless otherwise noted. All piecing is done with right sides together using a ½" seam allowances unless otherwise specified.

CUT THE FABRICS

From the green embossed velvet, cut:
- 7—4×57" strips, enough 2½"-wide strips to total 6½ yards
- 6 leaves

From the ivory velvet, cut:
- 3—4×57" strips
- 10 petals

From the ivory brocade fabric, cut:
- 1—48×65" piece for backing
- 3—4×57" strips

From the rose-stripe fabric, cut:
- 2—4×40" strips for the top and bottom borders
- 2—4×63" strips for side borders

From the interfacing, cut:
- 3 leaves

SEW THE QUILT

To piece the quilt top, alternately join green and ivory 4×57" strips. Alternate ivory brocade and ivory velvet in every other set. For shade variation, reverse the nap of alternate green velvet strips to run in the opposite direction.

Sew the 40"-long rose-stripe border strips to the top and bottom edges of the quilt top. Sew the 63"-long rose-stripe border strips to the sides of the quilt top.

FINISH THE QUILT

Smooth the pressed backing fabric on a large, flat surface, right side down. (Batting and backing should be larger than the quilt top.) Center and layer the batting over the backing. Layer the quilt top right side up on the batting. Baste the layers together with safety pins, working from the center of the quilt to the edges.

Using gold metallic thread and your sewing machine, machine-quilt a grid of 3" squares between the quilt borders.

For the binding strip, join the 2½"-wide green embossed velvet strips end to end, forming one long piece; press open the seam allowances. Press under ½" on one long edge of the binding strip. Sew the remaining long edge to the quilt back, raw edges even and mitering the corners. Trim the batting and backing even with the edges of the quilt front. Fold the binding to the quilt front, enclosing the raw edges and covering the stitching. Edgestitch the pressed edge of the binding to the quilt.

Use metallic thread to sew the fringe to the quilt top, aligning the top edge of the fringe with the border seams.

DECORATIVE FLOWER

Place two green leaves right sides together; place an interfacing leaf on top. Sew around the leaves, leaving the short edge open. Repeat to make three green leaves. Trim the seam allowances, turn right side out, and press. Use the gold metallic thread to narrowly zigzag-stitch a vein on each leaf. To gather the leaves, thread a needle with sewing thread and knot the ends together. Beginning at the point end on the back of the leaf, hand-sew running stitches in the zigzag stitches, taking care not to let the stitches show on the leaf front. Pull the thread to gather the leaf slightly; secure with a knot. For the flower base, arrange the green leaves in a circle with the short edges overlapping slightly in the center. Sew the leaves together for the flower base; set aside.

Sew the ivory velvet petals together in pairs, leaving the short edge open. Trim the seam allowances, turn right side out, and press. Use the gold metallic thread to narrowly zigzag-stitch a vein centered on each petal. To gather the petals, thread a needle with sewing thread and knot the ends together. Begin at the point end on the back of the petal and hand-sew running stitches in the zigzag stitches, taking care not to let the stitches show on the petal front. Pull the thread to slightly gather the petal; secure with a knot.

Arrange the ivory petals on the flower base, overlapping the short edges; sew the petals to the base. Cover the button form with gold metallic fabric, following the button manufacturer's instructions. Sew the button to the center of the flower and the flower to the corner of the quilt.
—*Designed by Lenny Houts*

Flower Petal/Leaf
Cut 6 green
Cut 10 ivory
Cut 3 interfacing

Harlequin Stockings

Shown on pages 57, 61, below, and opposite.
The finished stockings are 21½" long.

YOU WILL NEED

For each stocking:

Graph paper

⅝ **yard of embossed velvet or brocade fabric for stocking**

⅝ **yard of lining fabric**

¼ **yard of brocade or embossed velvet fabric for cuff**

¼ **yard of velvet for cuff lining**

½ **yard of coordinating fabric for bias binding**

⅛ **yard of gold metallic fabric for buttons**

Fabric marking pen

2—11×22" **pieces of lightweight cotton batting**

Gold metallic thread

Matching sewing threads

5—¾"-**diameter self-cover button forms**

16" **length of** ¼"-**diameter gold metallic twisted cording for hanging loop**

3"-**long tassel to match cuff**

INSTRUCTIONS

Note: *The yardages given for the stocking, cuff, cuff backing, and bias binding are enough to make two identical stockings. To make two stockings with reversed colors as shown, purchase ⅝ yard of both the embossed velvet and the brocade.*

Enlarge the stocking and cuff patterns, *page 68,* on graph paper. Add ½" seam allowances beyond the drawn lines and cut out the completed pattern pieces. Sew all pieces with right sides together using ½" seam allowances, unless otherwise noted.

EMBELLISH THE FABRIC

From the embossed velvet or brocade fabric, cut two 11×22" rectangles. Center the stocking pattern on the right side of one of the rectangles for the stocking front. Use the fabric marking pen to trace around the stocking pattern. Flip the pattern piece over and center on the second rectangle. Trace again for the stocking back. Do not cut out.

Place each fabric rectangle right side up on a piece of batting. Thread your sewing machine with gold metallic thread. Embellish the fabric inside the drawn stocking shapes by sewing along the embossed lines of the velvet or filling in the brocade shape with meandering stitching lines.

CUT THE FABRICS

Cut the embellished fabric along the drawn lines for the stocking front and back. Use the stocking pattern to cut two from the lining fabric. Use the cuff pattern to cut two from the brocade or embossed velvet fabric for the cuff front and back and two from the velvet for the cuff lining. Cut a 2×20" bias strip from coordinating fabric for the bias binding.

SEW THE STOCKING

Sew the stocking front to the back, leaving the top edge open. Trim the seams, and clip the curves. Turn the stocking right side out.

Sew the stocking lining pieces together, leaving the top edge open. Trim the seam allowances, and clip the curves; do not turn the lining right side out. Slip the lining into the stocking with wrong sides together. Machine-baste the raw edges together.

Sew the cuff front to the back at the lapel edge, sewing from the dot indicated on the pattern to the top edge. Sew the cuff front to the back at the opposite edge. Press the seam allowances open. Sew the cuff lining pieces together in the same manner and turn right side out. Slip the cuff lining into the cuff with right sides together. Beginning and ending at the dot indicated on the pattern, sew the lapel and bottom edges together. Trim the seams and turn the cuff right side out.

Slip the cuff onto the stocking, aligning the seams and keeping the raw edges even at the top edge. Baste the cuff to the stocking.

For the binding, press under ½" on one long edge of the bias strip. Beginning at the heel edge, sew the remaining long edge of the binding strip to the top edge of the stocking. Fold the binding to the inside of the stocking, enclosing the raw edges and covering the stitching. Blindstitch the pressed edge of the binding to the lining, trimming and folding in the short edges.

FINISH THE STOCKING

Cover five button forms with gold metallic fabric, following the button manufacturer's instructions.

For the cuff lapels, fold back the corners of the cuff so the velvet lining shows. Sew the lapels in place with a covered button. Sew another button at the lowest point of the cuff; slip the tassel over the button.

For the hanging loop, fold the gold metallic twisted cording in half. To secure the ends, wrap them together with a fabric scrap and sew back and forth over the scrap. Position the hanging loop over the lapel seam of the cuff, with the fold of the hanging loop about 2¼" above the stocking. Sew the loop to the cuff with two buttons, one just below the binding and one at the top of the folded lapel. Fold the wrapped ends of the loop to the lining side of the cuff and tack them in place.

—*Designed by Lenny Houts*

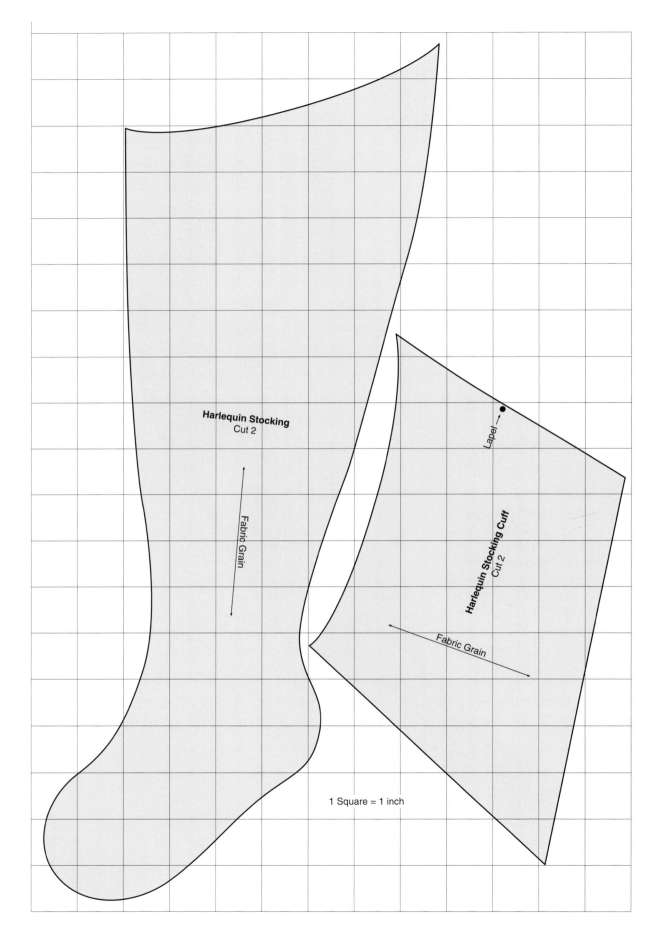

Harlequin Stocking
Cut 2

Fabric Grain

Harlequin Stocking Cuff
Cut 2

Lapel

Fabric Grain

1 Square = 1 inch

Rose and Pepper Berry Centerpieces and Wreath

Shown on pages 57–58 and right.

YOU WILL NEED

Ivory and taupe roses
Long-needle pine boughs
Seeded eucalyptus bunches
Rosemary bunches
Bunches of fresh pepper berries
Round glass container for the small centerpiece (right); long rectangular glass container for the candle centerpiece
3"-wide gold metallic ribbon
Florist's wire
5—15" tall white taper candles
Florist's foam and clay
Toothpicks
Fresh 30" (overall) noble fir wreath
Florist's water vials

SMALL CENTERPIECE

Fill the round glass container with florist's foam; soak the florist's foam in water. Cut and insert varying lengths of long-needle pine, sprigs of rosemary, and seeded eucalyptus—fanning out the greenery from the center of the arrangement.

Cut the roses to varying lengths and insert them into the florist's foam. Insert pepper berries in the centerpiece. Add more roses and greenery until you are pleased with the arrangement.

Make an eight-loop bow with gold ribbon and wrap the center with florist's wire. Tuck the ends of the florist's wire into the foam.

CANDLE CENTERPIECE

Cut enough florist's foam to fill the rectangular container. Firmly stick the florist's foam into the container with the clay. Use toothpicks to add several small pieces of foam to the original layer (to insert the candles at varied heights). Insert the tapers into the foam, making sure they are straight.

Fill the container with varying heights and varieties of greenery, as in the small centerpiece, *above*. Cut roses to varying heights and insert into the foam. Fill in the centerpiece with pepper berries and more greenery (avoid positioning greenery too close to the candles); add more roses if desired. Make and insert an eight-loop bow as described for the small centerpiece.

WREATH

Fill florist's vials with water and insert roses, rosemary, and seeded eucalyptus into the vials. Working from the top, wire the filled vials into the fresh wreath.

Make an eight-loop bow with gold metallic ribbon as described for the small centerpiece, except wire on two long tails to weave into the wreath. Cut a V in each tail.

TREE DECORATIONS

Fill florist's vials with water and insert roses, rosemary, and seeded eucalyptus into the vials. Wire the vials onto the tree. Fill in the tree with bunches of baby's breath (which do not need water). Add white or gold balls for a breathtaking Christmas tree.

—Designed by Lenny Houts

69

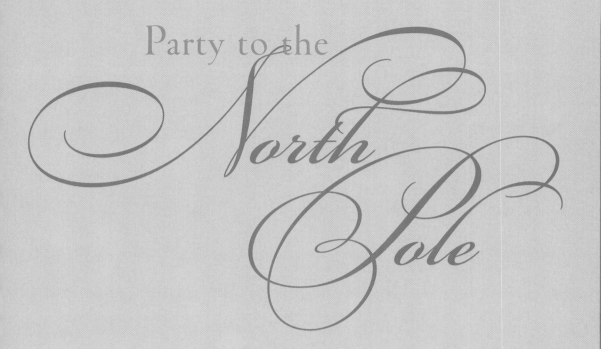

Party to the North Pole

Let it snow, let it snow, let it snow! That's the motif for this kids' party—where food and favors sparkle in white, silver, and blue. Don't be surprised if Frosty the Snowman shows up to join in the fun! Set the table glacial style with easy-to-make foam-plate cutouts, icy beverage holders, and glittering party favors. The great white North theme continues in cool, refreshing treats—from the Avalanche Gorp to the Blue Glacier Float to the Chocolate Graham-Peppermint Sandwiches. Instructions and recipes begin on page 76.

*L*ittle guests will shovel this scrumptious food onto their plates. Each icy place setting starts with a plastic plate topped with a layer of iridescent cellophane. Top it off with a cutout foam plate that looks like a hole broken through an icy pond. Fancy and tasteful treats are piled to satisfy as every hungry appetite. Wrap clear plastic tableware with icy blue beads for guests to take home. The kids will love ice cream floats that look as if they were plucked from deep snowbanks. Top the floats with whipped creamed snow, a bright red cherry, and a dusting of blue glacier crystals.

Snowball party favors will be gleefully opened by little party guests. Rubber balls and entertaining toys are wrapped in frosty blue and white crepe paper and secured with silver ribbons. Name tags with silver snowflakes direct gifts to each recipient.

ecorate your holiday tree with handmade North Pole-style ornaments (above). A frosty snowman tries to warm up with a pair of earmuffs made of pom-poms and pipe cleaners. Icicles drip with faux pearls and blue beads strung on wire. Snowflake ornaments are made using the plump ends of a cotton swab as a paintbrush. We guarantee that no two will be alike.

Hang an elegant snowball (right) above the table to set the wintry theme. It's as easy to make as rolling up a ball of fresh wet snow—or a ball of yarn. Wrap crystal white garland around a foam sphere and secure it with silver-studded organze ribbon.

Chocolate Graham-Peppermint Sandwiches

Shown on pages 71–72 and below.

YOU WILL NEED

1   cup canned vanilla frosting

6   tablespoons finely crushed candy canes or striped round peppermint candies

1   box of chocolate graham crackers

INSTRUCTIONS

Stir together frosting and crushed candies in a small mixing bowl. Break each chocolate graham cracker into halves. Spread frosting mixture on the unsugared side of a graham cracker half. Top with the remaining halves, sugared side to the top.

Blue Glacier Float

Shown on page 71 and below.

YOU WILL NEED

Blue bubble-gum flavored soda pop

Vanilla ice cream

Whipped topping

Blue sugar crystals

Maraschino cherries

INSTRUCTIONS

Scoop ice cream into Cracked-Ice Cups, *page 77.* Pour blue soda over ice cream. Top with whipped topping. Sprinkle sugar over topping, and place a cherry on top.

Snowman and Mitten Sandwiches

Shown on page 71–72 and below.

YOU WILL NEED

White bread

Peanut butter

Whipped cream cheese

Squeezable red raspberry jam

Dried blueberries

INSTRUCTIONS

Use cookie cutters to cut out snowman and mitten shapes from bread. Carefully spread peanut butter on the mitten-shape bread and cream cheese on the snowman shape bread. Make jam squiggles and dots on the mitten. Add jam for the snowman nose, mouth, and hat. Cut dried blueberries into quarters and use for eyes and buttons.

Avalanche Gorp

Shown on pages 71–72 and right.

YOU WILL NEED

1   12½-ounce package of bite-size white chocolate candies with chocolate cookie crumbs

1   7½-ounce package of white fudge-covered pretzels

1   12½-ounce package of yogurt-covered raisins

1   6-ounce package of dried blueberries

2   cups of bear-shape graham cracker cookies

2   cups of miniature marshmallows

2   cups of dried pineapple chunks

2   cups of dried roasted peanuts

1½   cups honey-roasted sunflower seeds

INSTRUCTIONS

Mix all ingredients in a large bowl. Store mix in a resealable plastic bag.

Cracked-Ice Cups

Shown on pages 71–72.

YOU WILL NEED

16-ounce foam cups
9-ounce clear plastic cups
Iridescent cellophane
Scissors

INSTRUCTIONS

To shape the foam cup, use scissors to cut down at an angle from the rim. Continue working around the cup, cutting out triangles until the entire rim is removed. Place a rectangle of cellophane, measuring about 4½×11½", over the base of a clear cup and hold it around the sides of the cup. Place the cellophane-wrapped cup into the cut foam base, working with the cellophane so it stick out slightly between the triangle cuts.
—*Designed by Heidi Boyd*

Cracked-Ice Plates

Shown on pages 71–72 and opposite.

YOU WILL NEED

Foam plates
Clear plastic plates
Iridescent cellophane
Crafts knife

INSTRUCTIONS

Place the foam plate on a protected work surface. Use the crafts knife to cut away triangles that start inside the rim of the plate and extend to the center of the plate. Continue working around the plate, creating a jagged starlike shape. Cut two squares of cellophane about 2" larger than the plates. Place the cellophane squares over the clear plastic plate and then place the cut foam plate on top of the cellophane.
—*Designed by Heidi Boyd*

Tableware Bracelet Favors

Shown on pages 71–72 and opposite.

YOU WILL NEED

Clear plastic tableware
Silver elastic cord
Red, blue, white, clear, and
  silver beads
Plastic animal or vehicle
  charm beads
Silver rimmed round tags
Dotted iridescent cellophane

INSTRUCTIONS

For each bracelet, cut an 8" length of silver elastic cord. Thread the beads on the cord with the charm bead in the center. String enough beads to fit comfortably around a child's wrist, approximately 4" to 5". Add a round tag at one end of the beads and knot the cord ends together.

Cut two 4" squares of cellophane for each set of tableware. Layer the squares and fold them diagonally into a triangle. Stack a spoon on a fork and wrap the folded edge of the cellophane triangles around the tableware at the top of the handles. To hold the cellophane in place, double-wrap the bracelet around the tableware and cellophane, pushing it up near the top of the handle.
—*Designed by Heidi Boyd*

Snowball Party Favors Centerpiece

Shown on page 71, 75, and left.

YOU WILL NEED

White and light blue crepe
  paper streamers
Small ball
Tiny toys and candies
Wired snowflake garland
Silver curling ribbon
Merchandise labels
Blue and silver markers
Silver snowflake sequins
Crafts glue
Sheet of dotted iridescent
  cellophane
Large clear plastic bowl

INSTRUCTIONS

Start each snowball by wrapping a streamer around a small ball. Secure tiny toys and candies in the streamer as you wrap. Cut the streamer when the ball reaches 4" to 5" in diameter.

Cut a 10" length of snowflake garland and wrap it around the snowball, twisting the ends together. Wrap the silver curling ribbon around the snowball as if wrapping a present. Knot and curl the ends of the ribbon. Use a marker to edge the merchandise label. Write the child's name and glue a snowflake sequin on the front of the label. Hook the label onto one end of the garland.

After making a snowball favor for each child, line a large plastic bowl with a sheet of dotted iridescent cellophane. Arrange the snowballs over the cellophane and place on the party table.
—*Designed by Heidi Boyd*

Snowman Ornaments

Shown on pages 71, 74, and right.

YOU WILL NEED

For each ornament:

1½"- and 2"-diameter plastic foam
  balls
Toothpicks
Crafts glue
Sparkle flakes
Foam glue
Chenille stems: 6" length of thick
  red or gray for scarf, 1" length
  of orange for nose, and 2"
  length of red-and-white or
  blue for earmuffs
1 small black paper clip for mouth
Wire cutters
Pom-poms: 2 mini black for eyes,
  2 red for buttons, and 2 red
  or blue for earmuffs
Straight pins
8" length of silver elastic cord

INSTRUCTIONS

Pierce each plastic foam ball with
a toothpick to serve as a handle.
Coat one ball with crafts glue and
immediately sprinkle it with sparkle
flakes. Repeat for the second ball.
Remove the toothpicks. Glue the
balls together with foam glue.

When the glue is set, wrap the
thick red or gray chenille stem around
the snowman's neck for the scarf.
Fold the orange chenille stem in half;
wrap one half around the other about
¼" from the cut end, creating a nose
with one sharp point opposite the
fold. Poke the sharp end of the nose
into the center of the face up to the
wrap. For the mouth, open the black
paper clip and cut off the largest
section. Unfold the large paper clip
section and bend the ends at a 90-
degree angle. Push these ends into
the face just below the nose. Glue
the mini pom-pom eyes to the face
above the nose and the red pom-
pom buttons to the center front of
the body.

For the earmuffs, curve the red-
and-white or blue chenille stem to
fit over the head. Bend the ends and
insert them into opposite sides of
the head. Glue matching pom-poms
to the head, covering the ends of
the chenille stem. Use straight pins
to anchor the earmuffs while the
glue dries. For the hanging loop,
bring the ends of the silver elastic
cord together around the top of the
earmuffs; knot.

—Designed by Heidi Boyd

Beaded Icicle Ornaments

Shown on pages 71, 74, and below.

YOU WILL NEED

22-gauge wire
Assorted packages of white,
  clear, light blue, silver, and
  pearl beads
Assorted packages of silver, clear,
  light blue, and white sequins,
  including star, snowflake,
  and flower shapes
Acrylic crystal drops

INSTRUCTIONS

For each ornament,
cut an 8" length of
22-gauge wire. To
form the hanging
loop, bend the top
1½" of wire into a
loop. Twist and
wrap the wire
around itself to hold
it in place. Thread
the beads and
sequins onto the
wire, beginning
with the largest and
descending to the
smallest. Add one
of the crystal drops;
then bend up the
end of the wire and
twist it around itself
several times above
the drop crystal.
*—Designed by
  Heidi Boyd*

Coaster Snowflake Ornaments

Shown on pages 71, 74, and above.

YOU WILL NEED

For each ornament:

1 cork coaster
Acrylic paint: blue and white
Paintbrush
Iridescent glitter
Flat and round toothpicks
Cotton swabs
Large-eye needle
18" length of 1"-wide sheer blue ribbon
8" length of silver elastic cord

INSTRUCTIONS

Base-coat one side and the edges of the coaster blue; let the paint dry. To paint the snowflake, apply white paint to the toothpicks and cotton swabs. Lay the toothpick or swab, paint side down, on the coaster. Carefully remove the toothpick or swab from the coaster. To vary the design, use just the tip of a swab to make dots or use just a portion of the toothpick. Immediately sprinkle glitter on the wet snowflake. When the snowflake is dry, use a large-eye needle to make a hole through the center top of the ornament. For the hanging loop, thread the silver elastic cord through the hole. Bring the cord ends together and knot. Tie the ribbon into a bow at the base of the hanging loop.

—Designed by Heidi Boyd

Snowball Ornaments

Shown on page 71 and below.

YOU WILL NEED

For each ornament:

2"—diameter plastic foam ball
1 yard of iridescent or white garland
Crafts glue
Straight pins
24" length of ¼"-wide silver ribbon
10" length of 1"-wide iridescent ribbon
10" length of silver elastic cord
Snowflake sequin

INSTRUCTIONS

Cover the plastic foam ball with glue and then wrap the garland around the ball, changing directions and overlapping the garland to cover the ball completely. Push a straight pin through the ends of the garland and into the ball to secure.

When the glue is dry, wrap the ¼"-wide silver ribbon around the ball as if wrapping a present. Knot the silver ribbon around the center of the iridescent ribbon and the silver elastic cord. Tie the iridescent ribbon into a bow. For the hanging loop, thread a snowflake sequin onto one end of the elastic cord. Bring the cord ends together and knot.

—Designed by Heidi Boyd

Large Snowball Decoration

Shown on page 75.

YOU WILL NEED

6"—diameter plastic foam ball
Iridescent or white garland
Crafts glue
Straight pins
2½ yards of 1"-wide silver-edged iridescent ribbon
18" length of 1"-wide iridescent ribbon
Clear fishing line

INSTRUCTIONS

Cover the plastic foam ball with glue and then wrap the garland around the ball, changing directions and overlapping the garland to cover the ball completely. Push a straight pin through each end of the garland and into the ball to secure.

When the glue is dry, wrap the silver-edged iridescent ribbon around the ball as if wrapping a present. To hang the snowball, cut a long length of clear fishing line. Knot the silver-edged ribbon around the center of the iridescent ribbon and the fishing line. Tie the silver-edged ribbon into a bow. Bring the fishing line ends together and knot.

—Designed by Heidi Boyd

Christmas at the Cabin

Bring home the feeling of cabin comfort. Inspired by nature and all her beauty, the lodge look infuses rustic charm into holiday decorating. Reminiscent of the woods on a snowy day, a snow-tipped faux wreath (opposite) features hand-painted folk art ornaments and a twig bow. Pair it with a painted tool box that has pine boughs and pine cones painted on the sides. Fill the wooden box with fragrant pine clippings, pinecones, and golden glass balls. (opposite on table). Instructions begin on page 88.

*S*nuggle under a cushy crocheted afghan (opposite) in front of a crackling fire to watch the snow fill the landscape outside. A blend of red, green, and white combines the colors of the season—and looks great all year round. A soft-as-snow folk art appliqué pillow adds to the inviting scene. Rustic buttons accent the pillow corners, reinforcing the woodsy theme of the room, while providing comforting winter warmth.

Matching crackle-painted photo frame and wooden box (above) are trimmed with pine boughs and pinecones for wintry woodland accents. Fill the box with fresh greenery or fire starters. Slip a sepia-tone photo into the frame for an old-fashioned look.

olorful appliqué and blanket stitching create these soft felt future heirlooms (above). Easily assembled cabins with doors, chimneys, and heart-shape windows sit snugly among evergreen trees on a snowy day. A loop of grosgrain ribbon is used to hang each customized stockings for Santa to find and fill.

A wonderful sentiment for a wonderful season! "Christmas is Love" felt sampler features a hand-stitched heart with a bird- and birdhouse-filled tree. The dark-stained wooden frame features well-worn buttons at each corner.

"The woods are lovely, dark, and deep..." —so the Robert Frost poem goes. This penny-style table runner captures the woodland feel, with cutout trees, a wandering moose, stars, and hearts. The brown and green felt penny border competely surrounds the runner.

For a true lodge look, spell out your holiday sentiments in twigs! The letters to "Happy Holidays" are easily made from supple dogwood branches. Attached to a barn board (or weathered piece of wood), this plaque will wish the best to all this holiday season—with the flair of the woods!

Woodland Fun Wreath

Shown on page 81 and above.

YOU WILL NEED
18" artificial evergreen wreath
Accent Design star, house, and
   moon wooden cutouts
Crafters Edition wooden skate
   #524-0924 and sleigh #524-
   2292 and rusted-metal star
   #RM35055
Aleene's Premium-Coat Acrylics:
   Black 176 (BK), Burnt Umber
   185 (BU), Deep Mauve 104
   (DM), Hunter Green 188 (HG),
   and Yellow Ochre 184 (YO)
Paintbrushes: #16 flat, #4 flat, 10/0
   liner, and spatter brush or old
   toothbrush
220-grit sandpaper
Tack cloth
Stencils: ⅛" stripe, ⅛" check, and
   ¼" circle
Wedge-shaped cosmetic sponges
Epoxy
22-gauge wire
Wire cutters
Darice grapevine bow #2810-76
Aleene's True Snow

INSTRUCTIONS

With the large flat brush, base-coat all surfaces of the skate and the house, and the edge of the sleigh seat DM. Base-coat all surfaces of the moon and star YO. Use HG to base-coat the top and bottom surfaces of the sleigh seat. When the paint is completely dry, lightly sand each piece. Remove the sanding dust with a tack cloth.

With the large flat brush, paint the roof and logs on the house BU. Let the paint dry. Use the #4 flat brush and BK to add the windows and door. Thin BK with water to ink consistency; use the liner to paint wavy lines along the top and bottom edges of the logs, on the roof for shingles, and on the chimney for bricks. Dip the handle end of the liner brush into YO, and dot the doorknob.

Paint the top ½" of the skate HG. With the ⅛" stripe stencil, YO, and the sponge, add stripes to the front surface of the skate below the HG and angled across the heel and toe. Stencil HG stripes on the front surface of the moon. Stencil DM circles on the front surface of the star. Stencil YO checks around the edges of the sleigh seat.

Thin BK with water to ink consistency. Use the liner to add "stitch" lines around the moon, star, and skate. With a spatter brush or an old toothbrush, spatter (flyspeck) all the pieces.

When the paint is dry, epoxy the rusted-metal star to the moon. Wire the grapevine bow to the top center of the wreath. Wire the painted wood pieces on the wreath, referring to the photograph on *page 81* for placement. Apply snow randomly to the wreath and bow, following the manufacturer's instructions. Use the snow sparingly on the edges of the painted pieces. Thin the snow with water and lightly spatter the front surfaces of all the painted pieces.

When completely dry, make a wire loop at the top center on the back of the wreath.
—Designed by Bonnie Stephens

Felt Snowman Pillow

Shown on page 82.

YOU WILL NEED
Tracing paper
Paper-backed fusible adhesive
1—9×12" piece each of black,
   burgundy, and white felt
Scraps of gold and blue felt
Cotton fabric scraps: red-and-
   cream check, green print,
   green plaid, and brown print
Cotton embroidery floss: black,
   orange, red, and white
Pearl cotton: Size 5 white and
   burgundy
Embroidery needle
Scrap paper
Erasable fabric marker
½ yard of striped cotton fabric
Matching sewing thread
4—⅜"-diameter assorted buttons
4—1"-diameter assorted buttons
Polyester fiberfill

INSTRUCTIONS

From the black felt, cut a 6¾×10½" rectangle. From the burgundy felt, cut a 5¼×9" rectangle.

Trace the pattern shapes, *opposite,* onto the paper side of the fusible adhesive, leaving ½" of space between the shapes. Cut the shapes out about ¼" beyond the drawn lines. Following the manufacturer's instructions, fuse the snowman on the white felt; the moon on the gold felt, the birds on the blue felt; the scarf on the red-and-cream check; the large tree on the green print; the small tree on the green plaid, and the trunk on the brown print. Cut out the pieces and remove the paper backing.

Referring to the photograph on *page 82,* arrange the snowman, scarf, trees, trunk, and moon on the burgundy rectangle, and fuse. Use one strand of white floss to make random straight stitches around the snowman. Use red floss to stitch around the scarf and small tree. Use

Ooh Starry Nights

black floss to straight stitch around the moon and the large tree, to make running stitches for the mouth, and to make French knots for the eyes. Straight stitch the carrot nose with orange floss.

Practice writing the lettering on scrap paper, referring to the pattern, *above*. Use the erasable marker to write the lettering in the top left corner of the burgundy rectangle. Use one strand of white pearl cotton to backstitch over the marker lines. Use one ply of white floss to randomly stitch the stars on the burgundy rectangle. Sew the 3/8"-diameter buttons on the center front of the snowman.

Center the burgundy rectangle on the black rectangle. Use two strands of white pearl cotton to make running stitches 3/16" from the edges of the burgundy rectangle. Arrange the birds on the layered rectangles and fuse. Use black floss to make a French-knot eye on each bird.

From the striped fabric, cut two 10×14" rectangles for the pillow front and back.

Center the layered rectangles on one striped rectangle. Use burgundy pearl cotton to blanket-stitch the layered black felt rectangle to the pillow front. Sew a 1"-diameter button to the pillow front at each corner of the black rectangle.

With right sides together, sew the pillow front to the back, using 1/2" seam allowances and leaving an opening on one side for turning. Clip the corners and turn right side out. Stuff the pillow firmly with fiberfill and slip-stitch the opening closed.
—*Designed by Sandy Dye*

Twig Holiday Greeting Sign

Shown on page 87.

YOU WILL NEED

2 to 3 fresh dogwood branches
or other pliable twigs
Twist ties
Assorted cylinders for shaping
twig letters around (bottles,
markers, etc.)
Pruning shears
Picture-frame wire
Wire cutters
5×24" piece of barn board
Epoxy

INSTRUCTIONS

Use pruning shears to cut the
dogwood branches into twigs of
assorted lengths to create letters and
parts of letters. Curl some of the cut
twigs around cylinders to create the
curved parts of the letters; use the
twist ties to hold the curved twigs
in shape for a day or two.

Cut picture-frame wire into 4" or
5" lengths. Wrap the picture frame
wire in a criss-cross fashion around
the twigs where they touch to hold
each letter together. Wrap a piece of
wire around the top of the "I" so it
matches the style of the other letters.
Arrange and epoxy the letters on the
barn board.
—*Designed by Glenda Aldrich*

Christmas Is Love

Shown on page 85.

YOU WILL NEED

Tracing paper
Permanent black marking pen
1—9×12" piece each of ruby and
antique white felt
Felt scraps: black, cinnamon, cocoa
brown, denim, gray, gold,
plum, sage, and walnut brown
Crafts glue
Waxed paper
Straight pins or toothpicks
Cotton embroidery floss: black,
brown, dark green, gold, light
blue, light green, pale yellow,
and red
Size 5 red pearl cotton
Embroidery needles
Creative Beginnings brass charms:
birdhouse (9100), key (2200),
large heart (1217), small heart
(2933), spade (6241), star
(1018), and wheelbarrow (6246)
Frame with an 8×8" to 8×9½"
opening; mounting board
Assorted buttons

INSTRUCTIONS

Trace the heart pattern, *opposite,*
including the lettering, onto tracing
paper; cut out. Use a black marking
pen to darken the lettering. Trace the
remaining pieces and cut out.

From the antique white felt, cut
one heart. From black felt, cut one
roof. From the cinnamon felt, cut
one pot and one roof. From the
cocoa brown felt, cut one tree trunk.
From denim felt, cut one bird and
one birdhouse. From gray felt, cut
one moon birdhouse. From gold felt,
cut one star. From plum felt, cut one
birdhouse and one roof. From ruby
felt, cut a square or rectangle at least
1" larger than the mounting board
for the background and two birds.
From sage felt, cut one of each tree
branch. From walnut brown felt, cut
two birdhouses.

CHRISTMAS is LOVE

To transfer the lettering, tape the antique white heart over the heart pattern on a bright window or light box. Trace the lettering onto the felt heart with an erasable fabric marking pen. Use two plies of black floss to embroider the lettering with straight stitches and French knots.

Referring to the pattern, position the felt shapes on the heart, pin or glue, and stitch in the order that follows. For a neatly finished piece, use glue sparingly, squeezing a small amount onto a piece of waxed paper. Dip the point of a straight pin or toothpick into the glue and dot the glue onto the back of the felt shape; place the shape in position.

Position the tree branches on the heart and center the trunk over the branches. Place the star at the top of the trunk and the pot at the bottom, slightly overlapping the trunk. Use one strand of matching floss to blanket-stitch the star, trunk, and pot to the heart and to backstitch a rim line on the pot. Use two plies of light green floss to embroider the branches to the heart, making random straight stitches resembling pine needles. Use two plies of red floss to make French knots along the branches.

Pin or glue the birdhouses and roofs from the branches, layering and overlapping the pieces. Use one ply of black floss to blanket-stitch the moon birdhouse to the bottom birdhouse, sewing through all layers. Use contrasting floss colors to backstitch a tiny heart on one birdhouse, to stem-stitch a moon on a second birdhouse, and to make French knots centered on the remaining birdhouses. Sew the roofs in place, making running stitches with one ply of black floss.

Pin or glue the birds in place. Using one ply of black floss, make French-knot eyes, and backstitch the legs, feet, and wing line. Make tiny running stitches from the lettering to the top bird.

Use two plies of dark green floss to backstitch a tree branch in the top right area of the heart, adding red French knots along the branch. Use matching floss to sew the star charm to the gold star, and to sew the birdhouse, wheelbarrow, and spade charms to the branches of the tree. Sew the small heart charm in the embroidered tree branch.

Center the heart on the ruby background and use red pearl cotton to blanket-stitch the heart to the background. Center the background on the mounting board and glue the edges to the back of the board. Insert the mounting board in the frame. Glue the assorted buttons and remaining charms to the corners of the frame.
—*Designed by Sandy Dye*

Woodland Penny Rug Runner

Shown on page 86.

YOU WILL NEED
Tracing paper
Kunin Rainbow felt: ⅜ yard of
    36"-wide cinnamon, ¼ yard of
    36"-wide cashmere tan, 29×12"
    pieces of hunter green, and
    19×12" piece each of cadet
    blue, cranberry, and leaf green
Size 8 pearl cotton: brown, gold,
    and green
Cotton embroidery floss: blue,
    brown, green, red
Embroidery needle

INSTRUCTIONS

Trace the patterns, *below and opposite,* onto tracing paper; cut out.

CUT THE FELT

From the cinnamon felt, cut:
- 1—8×19" piece for back
- 20 large tongues
- 1 moose
- 1 bear
- 2 pinecones
- 9 tree trunks

From the cashmere tan felt, cut:
- 1—8×19" piece for base

From the hunter green felt, cut:
- 20 small tongues
- 3 tall trees
- 2 short trees
- 1 tilted tree

From the cadet blue felt, cut:
- 3 stars

From the cranberry felt, cut:
- 5 hearts
- 1 fish stomach

From the leaf green felt, cut:
- 2 tilted trees
- 1 short tree
- 1 fish body

APPLIQUÉ THE TABLE RUNNER

Arrange the moose, bear, trees, tree trunks, fish, pinecones, hearts, and stars on the 8×19" cashmere tan base piece, referring to the diagram, *below,* for placement. Slip the tree trunks under the trees at different heights and overlap the pinecones and the fish pieces. Pin the shapes in place.

Use one ply of brown floss to whipstitch all the cinnamon felt shapes to the base. Use one ply of red floss to whipstitch the bottom edge of the fish stomach to the base. Use two plies of green floss to featherstitch along the bottom edge of the fish body and to make running stitches ⅛" from the outer edges of the fish body and from the edges of the trees. Use two plies of red floss and French knots spaced about ⅛" apart to secure the hearts to the base. Use two plies of blue floss to sew the stars to the base, alternating straight stitches with French knots.

To work couching stitch on the pinecones, use one strand of gold pearl cotton to make long straight diagonal stitches across the pinecones in opposite directions. Tack the stitches down where they intersect.

For the pine branches, use six plies of brown floss to stem-stitch three curved lines from the top center of the pinecones. Straight-stitch the pine needles with one strand of green pearl cotton.

Place a small tongue on each large tongue, aligning the straight edges. Use one strand of gold pearl cotton to blanket-stitch the rounded edges of the tongues together. There is no need to stitch across the straight edges.

FINISH THE TABLE RUNNER

Lay the base facedown on a flat surface. Arrange the tongues facedown on the edges of the cashmere tan base, overlapping them ½" and evenly spacing seven on each long side and three on each short end; pin them in place. Center the 8×19" cinnamon back piece on the wrong side of the base, covering the ends of the tongues; pin in place.

Blanket-stitch around the cashmere tan base with one strand of brown pearl cotton, sewing through all layers and catching the tongues in the stitching.

—*Designed by Robin Kingsley*

Penny Rug
**SMALL TONGUE and
LARGE TONGUE**
Cut 20 each

Woodland Penny Rug Runner Placement Diagram

Penny Rug
BEAR
Cut 1

Penny Rug
FISH BODY
Cut 1

Penny Rug
FISH STOMACH
Cut 1

Penny Rug
HEART
Cut 5

Penny Rug
TALL TREE
Cut 3 hunter green

Penny Rug
SHORT TREE
Cut 2 hunter green
Cut 1 leaf green

Penny Rug
TILTED TREE
Cut 1 hunter green
Cut 2 leaf green

TREE TRUNK
Cut 9

Penny Rug
MOOSE
Cut 1

Penny Rug
PINECONE
Cut 2

Penny Rug
STAR
Cut 3

Snowy Houses Christmas Stockings

Shown on page 84.

YOU WILL NEED
Graph paper
Tracing paper
½ yard *each* of 36"-wide green and red felt
3—9×12" pieces of antique white felt
2—9×12" pieces of black felt
1—9×12" piece *each* of gray and brown felt
½ yard each of green and red cotton fabric for lining
Cotton embroidery floss: black and off-white
Embroidery needle
Fabric glue
20" length of 1½"-wide black-and-white gingham ribbon
Scrap paper
White erasable marker
1 package of 8mm white sequins
1 package of rocaille beads
Sewing thread: white, red, and green
Black pearl cotton
12" length *each* of ⅝"-wide green and red grosgrain ribbon

INSTRUCTIONS
Enlarge the patterns, *pages 96–97,* on graph paper. Trace each full-size appliqué piece separately from the graph paper onto tracing paper. Cut out each pattern piece.

CUT THE FABRIC
From the green felt, cut:
• 2 stockings
• 1 large tree
• 1 small tree
• 1 large evergreen
• 1 small evergreen
• 2 two wreaths
From the red felt, cut:
• 2 stockings
• 1—3¾×5½" rectangle for house, and one heart

From the antique white felt, cut:
• 2 snow covers
• 2 roofs
From the gray felt, cut:
• 1—4¼×4½" rectangle for cabin
• 1 sidewalk
• 1—1×2¼" rectangle for cabin door
From the brown felt, cut:
• 3—1×4¼" strips for logs
From the black felt, cut:
• 1—1×7¼" strip for chimney
• 1—1×2¼" rectangle for house door
• 6—¾×1⅛" rectangles for windows and chimneys
• 1 heart
• 1 wreath center
• 2—½×1" rectangles for trunks
• 1 of each stepping-stone
From the green cotton fabric, cut:
• 2 stockings for lining, adding 1" to the top edge
From the red cotton fabric, cut:
• 2 stockings for lining, adding 1" to the top edge

APPLIQUÉ THE STOCKING
To position the felt pieces on the stocking, refer to the diagrams, *above* and *right*. Use three plies of black floss for embroidery stitches unless otherwise noted.

Position and pin a snow cover on the stocking front. Blanket-stitch the snow cover to the stocking front along the top edge only. There is no

need to sew the remaining edges yet—you'll do this when you sew the stocking front to the back.

Green Stocking. Blanket-stitch the house to the stocking front along the side and bottom edges. Pin the roof to the stocking front, overlapping the top edge of the house; slip two chimneys under the top edge of the roof. Glue the chimneys in place and blanket-stitch around the roof. Position the sidewalk on the snow cover, centering the top edge of the sidewalk along the bottom of the house. Work running stitches through all layers along the side edges of the sidewalk. Arrange the door, windows, heart, and wreath pieces on the house and glue in place. Arrange the large and small trees on the snow cover and slip a trunk under the bottom edge of each tree; glue the pieces in place.

Red Stocking. Position and pin the cabin and chimney on the stocking front with the cabin overlapping the chimney. Glue the chimney in place. Position the logs on the cabin and glue in place. Blanket-stitch the cabin to the stocking front along the side and bottom edges. Pin the roof to the stocking front, overlapping the top edge of the cabin. Blanket-stitch around the roof. Arrange the door, heart, and wreath pieces on the

cabin and glue in place. Position and glue the stepping-stones on the snow cover, beginning below the door. Arrange the large and small evergreens on the snow cover; glue in place.

FINISH THE STOCKINGS

Cut a 10" length of gingham ribbon. Pin the ribbon along the top of the stocking front, aligning the top edges and folding the raw edges to the back. Sew the ribbon to the stocking along the long edges.

To personalize the stocking, use the erasable marker to write the desired name across the stocking front and to draw smoke coming from the chimney below the name. Use four plies of off-white floss to work running stitches over the marker lines.

Arrange the sequins on the stocking front, referring to the photograph for placement. Mark the position of each sequin with the erasable marker. To attach the sequins, thread the needle with white thread; knot the ends. Bring the needle through the felt to the front of the stocking. Insert the needle through the sequin and a rocaille bead. Return through the sequin and the felt; knot the thread.

Center the stocking front on the stocking back; pin together. Use black pearl cotton to blanket-stitch the stocking front to the stocking back, leaving the top edge open. For the hanging loop, fold a 12" length of ⅝"-wide grosgrain ribbon in half. Sew the ends to the inside of the heel corner of the stocking front.

With right sides together, sew the lining front to back using ¼" seam allowances. Do not turn the lining right side out. Clip curves and press under 1" to the wrong side of the lining. Slip the lining inside the stocking with wrong sides together. Whipstitch the lining to the stocking at the top edge.
—*Designed by Connie Matricardi*

Pine Bough Box and Frame

Shown on page 83.

The frame is 10¾×12½". The box is 9×4¾×5¾".

YOU WILL NEED
10¾×12¾ Walnut Hollow wooden frame with a 5×7 opening
9×4¾×5¾" wooden box with handle
100- and 150-grit sandpaper
Tack cloth
Wood sealer
Delta Ceramcoat Acrylic Paints: Dark Brown 2053 (DB), Magnolia White 2487 (MW), Maple-Sugar Tan 2062 (MS), Palomino Tan 2108 (PM), Pine Green 2526 (PG), and Trail Tan 2435 (TT)
Paintbrushes: 1" flat, #10 or #12 flat, #3 round, #1 liner, and a small stiff stencil brush
Crackle medium
Tracing paper
Matte-finish varnish

INSTRUCTIONS

Sand all surfaces of the frame and box with 100- and then 150- grit sandpaper. Remove the sanding dust with a tack cloth. Apply wood sealer to all surfaces and let the sealer dry. Sand again with 150-grit sandpaper, and wipe clean with a tack cloth.

Base-coat only the front surface of the frame and box DB. When the base coat is dry, apply a coat of crackle medium to the painted front surfaces, following the manufacturer's instructions. Let the medium dry for the specified amount of time. Apply TT to the crackled surfaces. Let the paint dry.

Base-coat all remaining surfaces PG, including the inside edges of the frame opening and the handle of the box.

Trace the patterns, *page 98.* Transfer the pattern to the top left corner of the frame and the front of the box.

Use DB to paint the branches and to pounce on the pinecone area. Highlight along the bottoms of the branches with PM. Use the liner brush and PG to paint the needles. Mix PG with MW, and paint more needles. Mix MS and PM, and paint the petals on the front pinecone. Mix a little DB with MS, and paint the petals on the back pinecones. Highlight the ends of the petals with MW. To suggest snow, paint MW along the tops of the branches, and pounce it along the top edges of the pinecones. Lightly pounce MW on the needles.

Apply one or more coats of matte-finish varnish to all surfaces. Allow each coat to dry thoroughly.
—*Designed by Pat Olson*

Snowy Houses Christmas Stockings

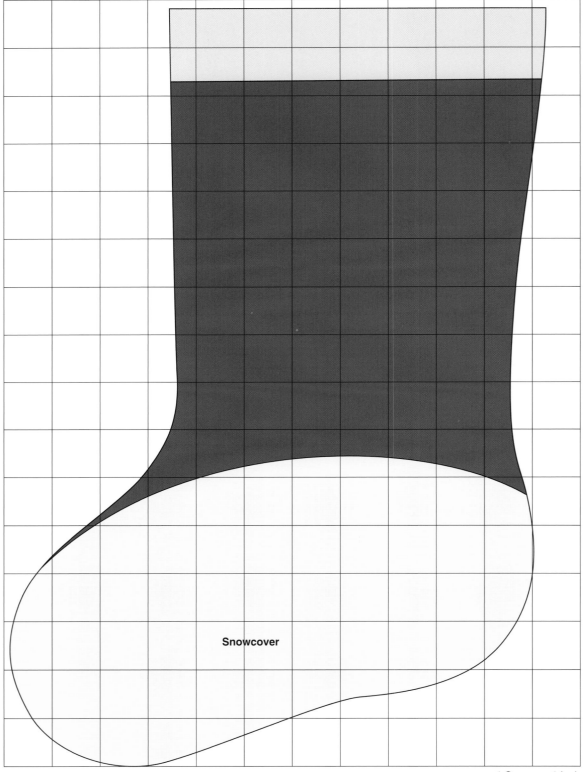

Snowcover

1 Square = 1 Inch

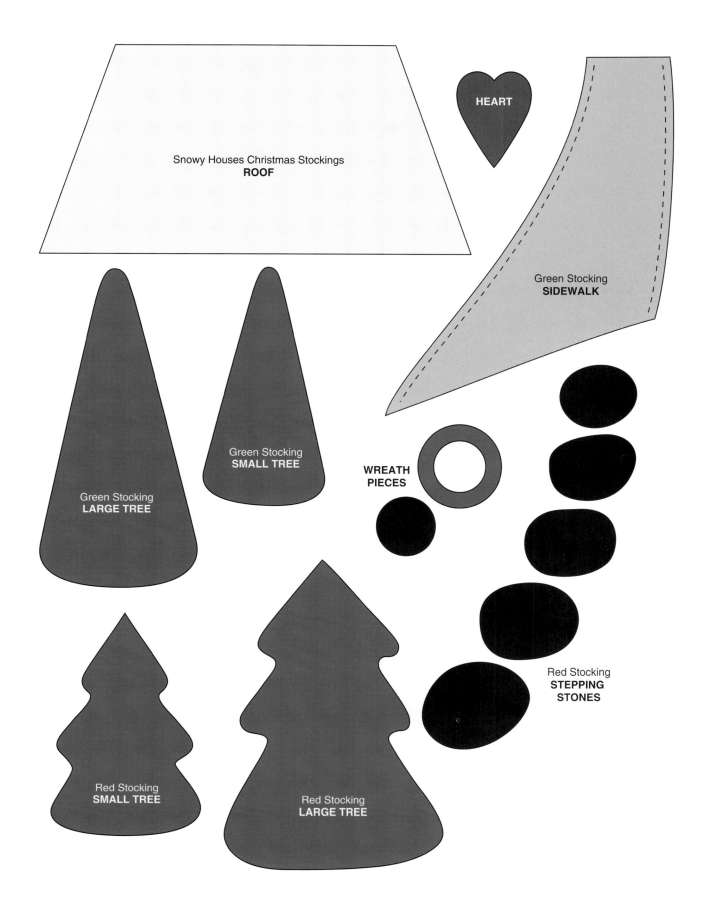

Snowy Houses Christmas Stockings
ROOF

HEART

Green Stocking
SIDEWALK

Green Stocking
SMALL TREE

Green Stocking
LARGE TREE

**WREATH
PIECES**

Red Stocking
**STEPPING
STONES**

Red Stocking
SMALL TREE

Red Stocking
LARGE TREE

Pine Bough Frame

Pine Bough Box

Holiday Cheer Afghan

Shown on page 82.

The finished afghan measures approximately 44×63 inches.

YOU WILL NEED

Red Heart Super Saver yarn

  21 oz. Holly & Ivy (967)— Color A

  18 oz. Burgundy (376)—Color B

  16 oz. Aran (313) —Color C

Size 15/N (9.00mm) aluminum crochet hook or size needed to obtain gauge

Size 8/H (5.00mm) aluminum crochet hook

GAUGE

Using two strands of yarn held together and larger hook, 14 sts = 5"; rows 5–16 = 5½"

CROCHET ABBREVIATIONS

Ch	chain
Dc	double crochet
Rep	repeat
RS	right side
Sc	single crochet
Sk	skip
Sl st	slip stitch
Sp	space
St(s)	stitch; stitches
WS	wrong side

STITCHES

Shell	3 dc in next st
V-stitch	in next st (dc, ch 1, dc)

Note: Using a double strand of yarn throughout, the afghan is worked in horizontal stripes.

INSTRUCTIONS

Using one strand each of Colors A and B, ch 166.

Row 1 (RS): Sc in 2nd ch from hook; * ch 1, sk 1 ch, sc in next ch; rep from * across; turn.

Row 2: Ch 1, sc in first sc; * ch 3, sk (ch-1 sp, sc, ch-1 sp), sc in next sc; rep from * across; turn.

Row 3: Ch 1, sc in first sc; * ch 1, sc in next ch-3 sp, ch 1, sc in next sc; rep from * across; turn.

Row 4: Rep Row 2. Fasten off.

Row 5: With the RS facing, join one strand each of Colors A and C with a sl st in first sc. Ch 3 (counts as dc), dc in same sc as joining. * SC in next ch-3 sp, shell in next sc; rep from * across ending sc in last ch-3 sp, 2 dc in last sc. Fasten off.

Row 6: With the WS facing, join one strand each of Colors A and B with a sl st in first dc. Ch 1, sc in same dc as joining. * Ch 3, sc in center dc of shell; rep from * across ending ch 3, sc in last dc; turn.

Row 7: Rep Row 3.

Row 8: Rep Row 2.

Rows 9–10: Rep rows 7–8. After Row 10, fasten off.

Row 11: With the RS facing, join a double strand of Color C with a sl st in first sc. Ch 1, sc in first sc; * V-st in next ch-3 sp, sc in next sc; rep from * across. Fasten off.

Row 12: With the WS facing, join one strand each of Colors A and B with a sl st in first sc. Ch 4 (counts as dc, ch 1), sc in next ch-1 sp; * ch 1, dc in next sc, ch 1, sc in next ch-1 sp; rep from * across ending ch 1, dc in last sc; turn.

Row 13: Ch 1, sc in first dc; * ch 1, sc in next sc, ch 1, sc in next dc; rep from * across; turn.

Row 14: Rep Row 2.

Row 15: Rep Row 3.

Row 16: Rep Row 2. Fasten off.

Rows 17–88: Rep rows 5–16 for six times more.

Rows 89–93: Rep rows 5–9. After Row 93, fasten off.

BORDER

With the RS facing, using larger hook, join a double strand of Color C with a sl st in first sc of Row 93.

Rnd 1: Ch 1, (sc, ch 2, sc) in same sc as joining for first corner. For the first side (parallel to the crocheted rows), * ch 1, sk next ch-1 sp, sc in next sc; rep from * across ending ch 1, sk last ch-1 sp, (sc, ch 2, sc) in last sc for 2nd corner. For the second side (perpendicular to the crocheted rows), work along the ends of the rows, counting the sc rows as 1 st and the dc rows as 2 sts. (Ch 1, sk 1 st, sc in next st) across to corner, ch 1 sk 1 st, in first ch of the foundation ch (sc, ch 2, sc) for 3rd corner. For the third side (along the foundation chain), (ch 1, sk 1 ch, sc in next ch) across ending ch 1, sk 2 ch, (sc, ch 2, sc) in last ch for 4th corner. Work the fourth side in the same manner as the second, ending ch 1, sk 1 st, join with a sl st in first sc; turn.

Rnd 2: With the WS facing, ch 1; * sc in next ch-1 sp, ch 1; rep from * around working (sc, ch 2, sc) in each corner ch-2 sp. At end, (sc, ch 2, sc) for corner, ch 1, join with a sl st in first sc; turn.

Rnd 3: Ch 4 (counts as dc, ch 1), sk next ch-1 sp and sc; * in the ch-2 sp of first corner (dc, ch 1, dc, ch 2, dc, ch 1, dc), (ch 1, sk next sc, dc in next ch-1 sp) around working rem corners as for the first. At end, ch 1, join with a sl st in 3rd ch of beg ch-4. Fasten off.

Rnd 4: With the RS facing and smaller hook, join one strand each of Colors A and B in a ch-1 sp in center of either side. * Ch 2, sk next dc, sl st in next ch-1 sp; rep from * around working (sl st, ch 3, sl st) in ch-2 sp of each corner. At end, ch 2, sk last dc, sl st in same ch-1 sp as joining. Fasten off.

Weave in loose ends on WS.

—Designed by Katherine Eng

Holiday

Bold & Bright

Go for the bold with your holiday decor! The royal court inspired our jewelry box of colors for the holidays. Ruby, sapphire, amethyst, and peridot jewel tones make up table settings fit for a king and queen. Dot-etched glass plates on silver chargers ornamented with faux rubies (right) sit upon amethyst-hued place mats with an elegant jewel drop that hangs from one end. The jewel-studded napkin holder matches the hand-painted blue stemware that is etched on the base and anointed with gold paint. A velvet jester stocking filled with candy canes makes a perfect party favor. Instructions begin on page 104.

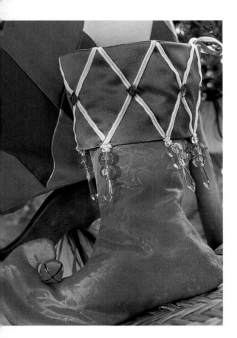

Catapult your holiday party into a tumble of color. Whimsical multicolored court jester-inspired chair covers (opposite) magically transform straight-back chairs into seats of royal distinction. Covers are made from a collage of fabrics stitched together like a quilt top—ending in a perfect point with a jeweled tassel. They slip over the chair like a glove on a hand!

Like a court dancer in midspin, our bejeweled tassel ornaments (opposite) do triple duty as tree ornaments, decorative place mats, and chair back tassels. They are made from ribbon, tulle, beads with faux gems, and wire.

Hang court jester stockings (bottom left) to add color and whimsy to your holiday gathering. You'll love every inch of this stocking—from its satiny jacquard cuff to its curled bell tip. Made from jewel-tone satin (we love fuchsia and purple together), and hung with strings of faux jewels, this stocking is pure fun!

Icicle Tassel Ornament

Shown on page 102 and below.

YOU WILL NEED

12" length of 28-gauge
copper craft wire
The Beadery products:
    4—6mm crystal round beads
    1—6mm gold large-hole
    round bead
    1—15×6mm sunflower bead cap
    1—23×15mm cushion bead
    1—18.5×12.5mm large-hole
    cushion bead
    1—18mm large-hole round bead
    1—32×9mm pendant bead
6" length of 18-gauge gold wire
Wire cutters

INSTRUCTIONS

Thread the pendant bead on the 28-gauge wire. Fold the wire in half, bringing the ends together with the pendant at the fold. Thread the wire ends through the 18mm round bead, small cushion bead, large cushion bead, bead cap, gold bead, and three crystal beads. Separate the wire ends

and thread each one through the remaining crystal bead from opposite directions. Twist the wires together at the top of the beads and create a small loop above the twisted area. Wrap the wires around the twisted area; trim the excess wire.

For the hanging loop, bend the 18-gauge wire into a fancy S-shape. Thread the hanging loop through the small loop at the top of the beads.
—*Designed by Margaret Sindelar*

Ribbon Tassel Ornament

Shown on page 102 and opposite.

YOU WILL NEED

4½×45" strip of sparkle netting
20—9" lengths of ⅛"-, ¼"-,
    and ⅜"-wide ribbons in
    assorted colors
12" length of cotton-wrapped
    craft wire
16mm jingle bell
Needle and sewing thread
The Beadery products:
    1—10mm crystal round bead
    1—22×13.5mm gold cushion
    bead
    1—40mm donut
    7—10mm acrylic faceted
    stones in assorted colors
Wooden beads: 12mm round and
    1¼" large-hole round
Wire cutters
Thick crafts glue
6" length of 22-gauge colored wire

INSTRUCTIONS

To make the ribbon loops, fold the 9" lengths of ribbon in half. Space the ribbon loops about 1" apart along one long edge of the netting, and machine-baste the ribbon ends to the netting ¾" from the netting edge. Continue machine basting to the end of the netting. Pull the basting threads to tightly gather the top edge of the netting; knot the threads to secure.

Thread the jingle bell on the cotton-wrapped craft wire. Fold the wire in half and twist together above the bell. Wrap the gathered edge of the netting around the craft wire just above the jingle bell, beginning with the end opposite the ribbon loops. Use a needle and thread to secure the wrapped netting. Apply thick crafts glue to the gathered edge of the netting. Allow the glue to dry slightly and slip the donut over the wire and gathers. Then thread on the 1¼" round wooden bead, the gold cushion bead, and the 12mm round

Tassel-Tipped Place Mat

Shown on page 101 and below.

YOU WILL NEED

For each place mat:

18" square of fuchsia metallic fabric

18" square of fuchsia satin fabric

Matching sewing thread

Carpet thread

Large-eye needle

The Beadery products:

    1—6mm gold large-hole round bead

    1—15×6mm sunflower bead cap

    2—18mm large-hole round beads

    1—32×9mm pendant bead

INSTRUCTIONS

With right sides facing, sew the fabric squares together using ¼" seam allowances and leaving an opening on one edge for turning. Trim the corners, turn right side out, and press.

Thread the large-eye needle with carpet thread and knot one end. Working through the opening in the place mat, bring the thread out at one corner of the place mat. Thread the gold bead, bead cap, two round beads, and pendant bead on the needle. Return the needle back through all beads except the pendant bead to the place mat; knot securely on the inside of the place mat.

Slip-stitch the opening closed. Sew the fabric layers together diagonally from corner to corner.

—Designed by Margaret Sindelar

wooden bead. Separate the wire ends and thread each one through the crystal bead from opposite directions. Cut the wire ends even with the sides of the bead. Glue the faceted stones around the sides of the 1¼" round wooden bead.

For the hanging loop, thread the 22-gauge wire through the crystal bead. Bend the wire into a fancy S-shape.

—Designed by Margaret Sindelar

Ribbon-Topped Table Runner

Shown on pages 101 and 102.

YOU WILL NEED

½ yard of blue satin fabric

½ yard of blue cotton fabric

½ yard of fleece or batting

Fabric marking pencil

Matching sewing threads

1½ yards each of 1"-wide purple, green, and royal blue velvet or satin ribbons

1½ yards each of ⅛"- or ¼"-wide bright pink, lime-green, and purple satin ribbons

1½ yards each of ⅜"-wide purple, green, and royal blue velvet ribbons

2¾ yards of 1"-wide royal blue satin ribbon for binding

INSTRUCTIONS

Use the fabric marking pencil to draw a 14×32" rectangle centered on the right side of the blue satin fabric; *do not* cut out now. To draw a diamond

Continued

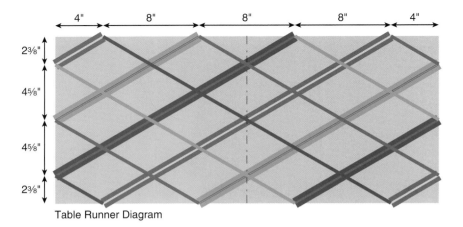

Table Runner Diagram

grid on the front of the satin fabric, refer to the diagram, *page 106,* and beginning 4" from one short edge, make marks 8" apart along both long edges of the rectangle. Beginning 2⅜" from one long edge, make marks 4⅝" apart along both short edges of the rectangle. Draw lines connecting the marks to create the diamond grid.

Place the satin fabric, right side up, over the fleece on a flat surface. Pin the layers together. Referring to the photograph, *pages 101 and 102,* for color placement ideas, center a 1"-wide ribbon with a ⅛"- or ¼"-wide ribbon atop over each drawn grid line in one direction. Sew the ribbons in place. Sew the ⅜"-wide velvet ribbons over the drawn grid lines in the opposite direction.

With wrong sides together, smooth the ribbon-trimmed satin fabric over the blue cotton fabric. Pin the layers together and machine-baste ¼" inside the drawn lines of the rectangle. Cut through all layers on the drawn lines.

To bind the table runner, fold the 1"-wide blue satin ribbon over the edges of the runner. Edge-stitch the ribbon in place, mitering the corners and taking care to catch both long edges of the ribbon in the stitching.
—*Designed by Margaret Sindelar*

Jewel Ribbon Napkin Ring

Shown on page 101 and right.

YOU WILL NEED

8" length of 1"-wide green velveteen ribbon
8" length of ¼"-wide bright pink satin ribbon
2½×8" strip of wire mesh
1¾×2½" brass jewelry finding
The Beadery 40×30mm acrylic faceted stone
Crafts glue and epoxy

INSTRUCTIONS
Center and glue the bright pink satin ribbon on the green velveteen ribbon. Place the ribbons facedown and centered on the wire mesh strip. Fold the wire mesh to the back of the ribbons. Bend the mesh-covered ribbons into a circle, overlapping the ends; glue the overlapped area to secure. Epoxy the jewelry finding to the ribbon circle, covering the overlapped ends. Epoxy the faceted stone to the jewelry finding.
—*Designed by Margaret Sindelar*

Diamond Chair-Back Slipcover

Shown on pages 102 and 103.

YOU WILL NEED

Quilter's template plastic or tracing paper
Tape measure
Brown kraft paper
¼ yard each of 12 solid fabrics in assorted shades of royal blue, purple, fuchsia, and lime-green
¾ yard of fuchsia fabric for back
¾ yard of fuchsia lining fabric
Matching sewing thread
5½×45" strip of sparkle netting
20—10" lengths of ⅛"-, ¼"-, and ⅜"-wide ribbons in a variety of colors
12" length of cotton-wrapped craft wire
16mm jingle bell
Needle and sewing thread
The Beadery products:
    1—10mm crystal round bead
    1—22×3.5mm gold cushion bead
    1—40mm donut
    7—10mm acrylic faceted stones in assorted colors
Wooden beads: 12mm round and 1¼" large-hole round
Wire cutters
Thick crafts glue

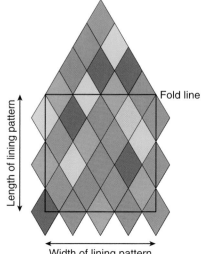

Length of lining pattern

Fold line

Width of lining pattern

INSTRUCTIONS

Trace the diamond pattern, *page 108,* onto template plastic or tracing paper; cut out. For the lining pattern, measure the width and height of your chair back. Add 3" to the width and 1½" to the height for ease and seam allowances. Decrease the height if a shorter slipcover is desired. Use these measurements to cut a pattern from brown kraft paper; cut out the pattern piece.

Sew all pieces with right sides together using ¼" seam allowances, unless otherwise noted.

CUT THE FABRICS

Use the diamond pattern to cut enough diamonds from the 12 various shades of fabric to piece fabric large enough for the slipcover. Our chair used 33 diamonds.

Use the lining pattern to cut two shapes from the lining fabric.

SEW THE SLIPCOVER

Referring to the diagram, *opposite,* arrange the diamonds beginning at one end with one diamond. Increase the number of diamonds in each subsequent row by one until the width accommodates the width of your lining pattern. Note the point where the required width begins; this is the fold line at the top of the chair back. Maintaining this minimum width, continue adding rows of diamonds until the length from the fold line to the bottom is large enough to accommodate the length of your lining pattern.

Sew the diamonds together in diagonal rows, carefully noting placement and direction of each diamond. Press the seam allowances in alternate directions from row to row. Sew the rows together.

Lay the pieced fabric on a flat surface. Position the lining pattern on the fabric with the top edge of the pattern at the fold line as shown in the diagram. Pin the pattern to the fabric. For the slipcover front, cut the pieced fabric along the side and bottom edges of the pattern; do not cut along the top edge of the pattern. Use the slipcover front as a pattern to cut one from the fuchsia fabric for the back.

Sew the slipcover front to the back, leaving the bottom edge open. Clip the corners, but do not turn.

Sew the slipcover lining pieces together, leaving the bottom edge open and an opening on one side for turning. Trim seam allowances; turn the lining right side out.

Slip the lining inside the slipcover with right sides together. Sew the lining to the slipcover at the bottom edges. Turn the slipcover and lining right side out through the side opening in the lining. Slip-stitch the opening closed. Tuck the lining inside the slipcover and press.

FINISH THE SLIPCOVER

To make the ribbon loops, fold the 10" lengths of ribbon in half. Space the ribbon loops about 1" apart along one long edge of the netting and machine-baste the ribbon ends to the netting ¾" from the netting edge. Continue machine basting to the end of the netting. Pull the basting threads to tightly gather the top edge of the netting; knot the threads to secure.

Thread the jingle bell on the cotton-wrapped craft wire. Fold the wire in half and twist together above the bell. Wrap the gathered edge of the netting around the craft wire just above the jingle bell, beginning with the end opposite the ribbon loops. Use a needle and thread to secure the wrapped netting. Apply thick crafts glue to the gathered edge of the netting. Allow the glue to dry slightly and slip the donut bead over the wire and gathers. Glue 10mm faceted stones around the middle of the 1¼" wooden bead; let the glue dry. Then thread on the 1¼" round wooden bead, the gold cushion bead, and the 12mm round wooden bead. Separate the wire ends and thread each one through the crystal bead from opposite directions. Twist the wire together at the top of the crystal bead.

Hand-sew the tassel to the wrong side of the slipcover point and trim the excess wire.

Slip the slipcover over the back of the chair with the pieced fabric to the front and fold the point over to the back.

—*Designed by Margaret Sindelar*

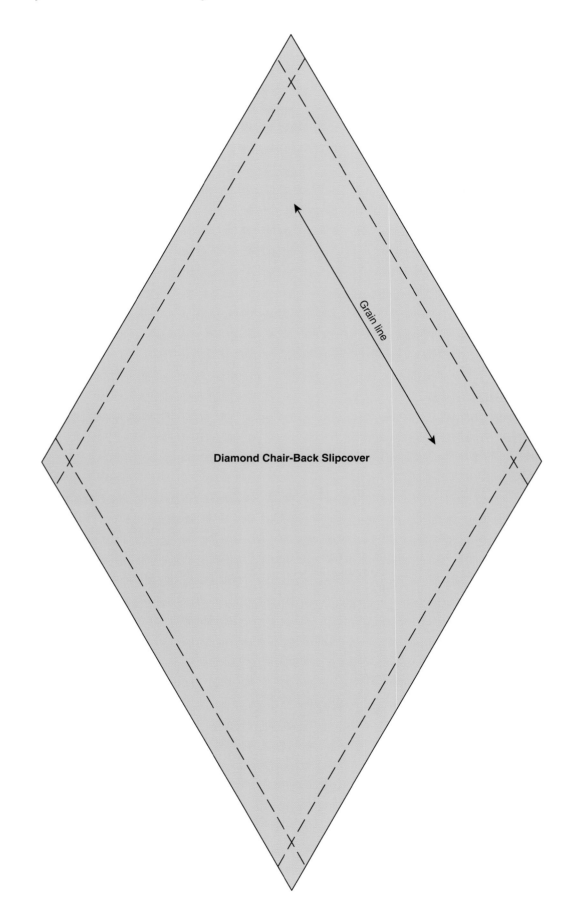

Diamond Chair-Back Slipcover

Grain line

Jester-Style Stocking

Shown on pages 102 and 103.

YOU WILL NEED

Graph paper

⅝ yard of fuchsia fabric for stocking front and back

⅝ yard of blue lining fabric

10×18" piece of purple satin fabric for cuff

½ yard of fleece

14×18" piece of fusible interfacing

Matching sewing threads

Fabric marking pencil

2¾ yards of ⅜"-wide fuchsia satin ribbon

2¾ yards of ¼"-wide pink velvet ribbon

The Beadery products:

    7—6mm crystal round beads

    7—18mm topaz large-hole round beads

    7—18mm rose quartz large-hole round beads

    7—32x9mm rose quartz pendant beads

    7—12mm Clearly Mosaics squares

Carpet thread; large-eye needle

Gem-Tac glue

1" red jingle bell

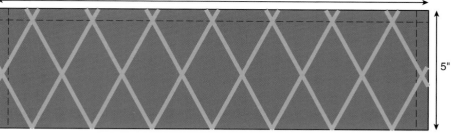

DIAGRAM 1

INSTRUCTIONS

Enlarge the stocking pattern, *page 111,* on graph paper; cut out. Sew all pieces with right sides together using ½" seam allowances, unless otherwise noted.

CUT THE FABRICS

Use the stocking pattern to cut two stockings from the fuchsia fabric for the front and back. From the lining fabric, cut two stockings for the lining front and back. From the fleece, cut one stocking for the stocking front and a 5×18" strip for the cuff. Cut one stocking from the interfacing for the stocking back.

SEW THE STOCKING

Machine-baste the fleece shape to the wrong side of the stocking front. Fuse the interfacing shape to the wrong side of the stocking back, following the manufacturer's instructions. Sew the stocking front to the back, leaving the top edge open (see Step 1, *page 110).* Trim the seam allowances, and clip the curves. Turn the stocking right side out.

With wrong sides facing, press the 10×18" cuff piece in half lengthwise to measure 5×18". Use the fabric marking pencil to draw a diamond grid pattern on the front of the cuff, referring to Diagram 1, *above.* Beginning at the center of the folded edge, draw 4½"-tall diamonds with the points 2½" apart. Unfold the cuff and machine-baste the 5×18" fleece strip to the wrong side of the cuff front along the raw edges. Center and sew the satin and velvet ribbons, layered in that order over the drawn lines, extending the ribbon ends slightly into the seam allowances and onto the cuff back.

Referring to Step 2, *page 110,* sew together the short edges of the cuff, forming a circle. Refold the cuff along the pressed fold, matching the raw edges and seams. Machine-baste the raw edges together. Slip the cuff onto the stocking, centering the cuff seam on the stocking back and keeping raw edges even (Step 3). Machine-baste the cuff to the stocking.

For the hanging loop, cut a 7" length each of satin and velvet ribbons. Center and sew the velvet ribbon on the satin ribbon. Fold the ribbons in half. With raw edges even, sew the ribbon ends to the top corner on the heel side of the stocking.

Sew the stocking lining pieces together, leaving the top edge open and a 4" opening on one side for turning (Step 4). Trim the seam allowances, and clip the curves; *do not* turn the lining right side out.

Slip the stocking and cuff inside the lining with right sides together (Step 5). Sew the stocking to the lining at the top edges (Step 6). Trim the seam allowances. Turn the stocking and lining right side out through the side opening (Step 7). Slip-stitch the opening closed (Step 8). Tuck the lining into the stocking.

Unfold the cuff from the stocking and sew through the stocking and lining layers ¼" from the top of the stocking (Step 9). Refold the cuff down over the outside of the stocking (Step 10).

To make a bead fringe, thread the large-eye needle with carpet thread and knot one end. Working from the wrong side of the cuff, bring the needle out at the bottom of one ribbon diamond. Thread the crystal round, topaz round, rose quartz round, and pendant beads on the needle. Return the needle back through all beads except the pendant bead to the cuff; knot on the wrong side of the cuff to secure. Repeat to make a bead fringe at the bottom of each ribbon diamond on the cuff.

Glue the Clearly Mosaics squares to the cuff at the intersections of the ribbon diamonds. Sew the red jingle bell at the tip of the stocking.

—Designed by Margaret Sindelar

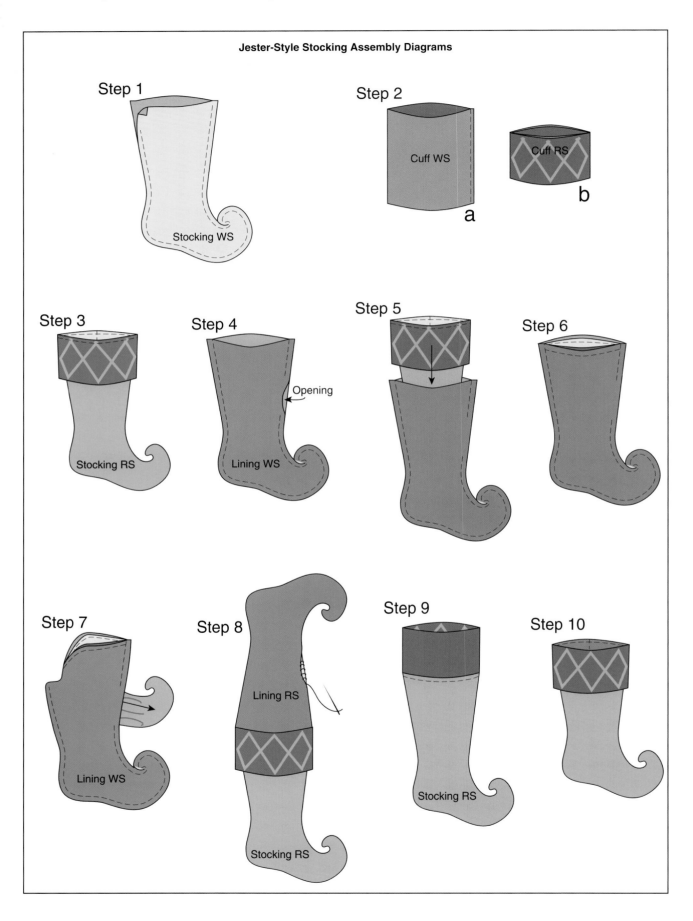

Jester-Style Stocking Assembly Diagrams

Step 1

Stocking WS

Step 2

Cuff WS

Cuff RS

a

b

Step 3

Stocking RS

Step 4

Opening

Lining WS

Step 5

Step 6

Step 7

Lining WS

Step 8

Lining RS

Stocking RS

Step 9

Stocking RS

Step 10

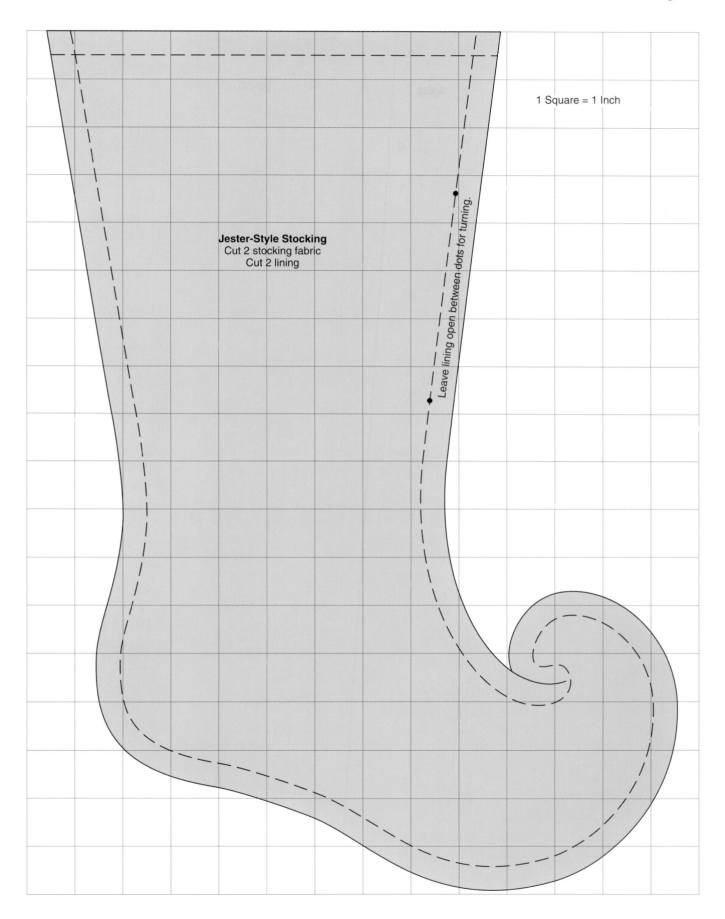

1 Square = 1 Inch

Jester-Style Stocking
Cut 2 stocking fabric
Cut 2 lining

Leave lining open between dots for turning.

Painted Stemware, Dinner Plate and Charger Plate

Shown on pages 101–102 and right.

YOU WILL NEED
Stemware with clear bases
Clear glass plates
Silver charger plates
Paint pens in black and gold
Self-adhesive paper
½"-diameter hole punch
Glass etching medium
4 pear-shape flat-back gems
Epoxy

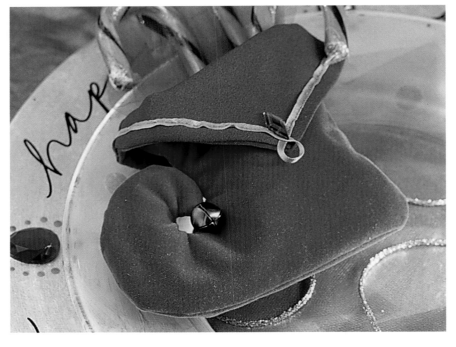

STEMWARE AND GLASS PLATE

Wash and dry each glass and clear glass plate. Punch out ½"-diameter circles from self-adhesive paper, using the hole punch. Remove the paper backing and randomly stick the circles onto the bottom sides of the plate rim and the bottoms of the stemware. (We used about 16 circles for each plate and five or six for each glass.) Following the directions for the glass-etching medium, etch the underside of the base of each glass and the bottom side of the rim of each plate. After the etching process is complete, remove the sticker circles.

To finish the etched stemware, use the gold paint marker to make graduating dots on the top of the base from the stem out. Refer to the diagram *opposite*. Let the paint dry. Hand-wash the glassware only.

CHARGER PLATE

Using the black paint pen, write "happy holidays" around the rim of the charger, leaving a space between words that is wide enough for a gem. Epoxy the four gems to the rim of the charger.

Add graduating gold dots around each gem, referring to the photograph, *page 101*. Let the epoxy and paint dry. Hand-wash only.

—Designed by Carrie Topp

Jester Stocking Favor

Shown on pages 101–102 and above.

YOU WILL NEED
Tracing paper
9×18" piece of hot-pink velveteen
9×18" piece of blue lining fabric
½ yard of ⅛"-wide lime-green satin ribbon
Matching sewing threads
2—18×9mm diamond-shape green rhinestones
Gem-Tac glue
12mm green jingle bell

INSTRUCTIONS

Trace the pattern, *opposite,* onto tracing paper and cut out. Sew all pieces with right sides together using ¼" seam allowances, unless otherwise noted.

CUT THE FABRICS

Use the stocking pattern to cut two from the velveteen for the stocking front and back and two from the lining fabric for lining front and back.

SEW THE STOCKING

Sew the stocking front to the back, leaving the top edge open (see Step 1, *page 110).* Clip the curves. Turn the stocking right side out. Finger-press the seams.

Sew the stocking lining pieces together, leaving the top edge open and an opening on one side for turning (Step 4). Clip the curves, but *do not* turn the lining right side out.

Slip the stocking inside the lining with right sides together (Step 5). Sew the stocking to the lining at the top edges (Step 6). Turn the stocking and lining right side out through the side opening (Step 7). Slip-stitch the opening closed (Step 8). Tuck the lining into the stocking and press. Then turn the stocking with the lining side facing out.

Beginning at the seam on the heel side, sew the ribbon to the lining side of the stocking ¼" from the top edge, leaving a loop at each point. Turn the stocking right side out again, and fold the top of the stocking (the lining) down to create the cuff. Glue a diamond-shape green rhinestone to the front and back points of the cuff. Sew the jingle bell to the tip of the stocking.

—Designed by Margaret Sindelar

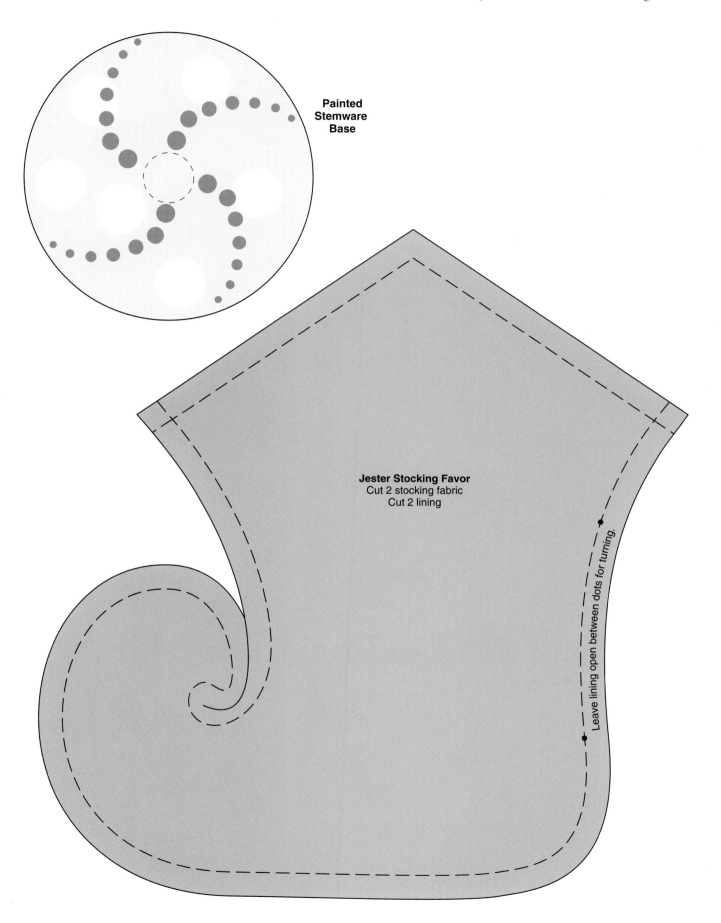

**Painted
Stemware
Base**

Jester Stocking Favor
Cut 2 stocking fabric
Cut 2 lining

Leave lining open between dots for turning.

Gifts for *Family & Friends*

Celebrate the holidays with handmade gifts from the heart. Family and friends (including beloved pets, of course) will treasure these gifts for many holidays. Playful felt pieces and colorful stitchery (opposite) make up a catnip-filled stocking for a favorite feline. For a favorite canine friend, see page 127 for a stocking that will have Fido sitting up and doing tricks. For young animal lovers on your list, sew a flock of friendly sheep (below). Instructions start on page 126.

*A*ll that glitters is not gold—and this centerpiece proves it. "Sew" four small bottles together with copper wire and string with beads in a glittery web to create a centerpiece that reflects your favorite person's decor. Just add colored beads or stones to the jars, insert tapered candles, and light up for instant holiday ambience!

Hand-painted stemware does double dining duty— it's both place card and wine glass. With festive holiday paint, a paintbrush, and a steady hand (we suggest putting on Christmas music to soothe and inspire you), you can transform plain stemware into custom crystal. The bowl of the stemware is personalized with your recipient's name and a brightly painted ornament; the base is painted in red and black stripes.

he perfect gift for the seamstress on your holiday list! Transform a vintage handkerchief into a colorful pin cushion (above). The plump center is stuffed with fiberfill to keep an assortment of pins within reach.

Samplers, dating from 16th-century Europe, add warmth and tradition to any home. Create a holiday heirloom by stitching a sampler (opposite) that bestows blessings upon all who enter your home. True to sampler style, diverse embroidery techniques achieve this time-honored classic to be enjoyed for many holidays to come.

ive the spa treatment to a friend who needs stress relief. (Make a skin-soothing bath mitt for yourself as well). Select a standard-size washcloth. Then, with a little terry-cloth origami and a few quick stitches, you have a magnificent mitt (opposite). Tuck a sented soap in the fold for the perfectly fragrant invitation to indulge in a steamy, relaxing, and invigorating bath.

Soap making is an art—and was an all-day affair for colonial women. Using a microwave oven, you can make gorgeous, scent-sational bars of soap in minutes. Pressed flowers from the garden, transparently suspended in glycerine soap, are enhanced with your favorite scents to make beautiful and soothing gifts for family and friends.

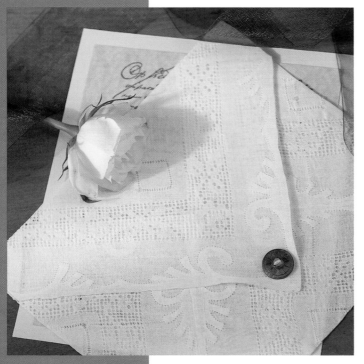

Special delivery! Here's an envelope everyone will be eager to open. A lace handkerchief is folded to make an elegant envelope that is the perfect vehicle for family photos and heartfelt holiday greetings.

nspired by the glories of nature, our flower- or dragonfly-topped sachets (opposite) bring the fresh scents of the garden to your dresser drawers and closets. Two matching cloth coasters are stitched together with ribbon, filled with fiberfill, and scented with rose petals, potpourri, or dried lavender buds. The handmade rose topping the sachet on the left is creatively crafted from ribbon. Simply too pretty to hide away, these garden-fresh sachets will add a decorative touch anywhere in the house.

Add elegance to your mantel with our white-on-white holiday stocking (below). Made from luxurious pristine white velvet and lined with snowy fabric, our stocking is topped with a creamy crocheted snowflake cuff. After the holidays are over, you may not want to pack away this stocking. Because the neutral color makes it a year-round decoration, you can hang it in a bedroom or bathroom—filled with fragrant lavender sprigs or mini bouquets of dried roses.

Here's a secret Santa treat! Stash special holiday goodies in our Santa candy holder. Start with a lidded jar and sculpt a friendly St. Nick from an easy-to-use, quick-drying clay product. With a paintbrush, add all of Santa's trademark features: rosy checks, twinkling eyes, and a happy, ho-ho-ho demeanor. The Santa candy holder unscrews at the waist to reveal a sweet-filled center.

Papier-Mâché Santa Gift Container

Shown opposite.

YOU WILL NEED

Celluclay instant papier-mâché

Dust mask

Resealable plastic bag

Glass jar with screw-on lid about 3½" tall, such as a bouillon jar

Round plastic container about 5" tall with a diameter similar to the glass jar

Plastic lid about 1" tall with a diameter smaller than the glass jar

Duct tape

Sculpting tools, such as toothpicks, a knitting needle, and a small thin-blade knife

Wire rack

Plaid Folk Art acrylic paint: Almond Parfait 705 (AP), Asphaltum 476 (AM), Basil Green 645 (BG), Christmas Red 958 (CR), Ivory White 427 (IW), Licorice 938 (LI), Pure Gold 660 (PG), Raw Umber 485 (RU), Taffy 902 (TA), and Teal Green 733 (TG)

Assorted paintbrushes, including flat, liner, and round

Antiquing medium

Paper towels; waxed paper

Acrylic matte-finish spray

Drill

Piece of artificial greenery

Crafts glue

SHAPING THE SANTA

Line the work area with waxed paper. For safety, wear a dust mask to avoid breathing papier-mâché dust. Mix half the package of the instant papier-mâché with water, following the manufacturer's instructions. Keep any unused papier-mâché mixture in a resealable plastic bag while you work and refrigerate the mixture in the bag for future use.

Remove the lid from the glass jar and set it aside. Moisten your fingers with water and apply a thin, even coat of the papier-mâché mixture to the sides and bottom of the jar, being careful not to get any mixture on the threads of the jar. Allow to dry.

Use thin strips of duct tape to secure and center the plastic container onto the top of the lid of the glass jar. Apply a thin, even coat of the papier-mâché mixture to the plastic container and the lid, keeping the mixture away from the threads of the lid.

For the boots, center the 1"-tall lid on the bottom of the glass jar with the open part of the lid against the jar. Secure with duct tape strips. Apply a thin, even coat of mixture to the sides and bottom of the boots.

When the mixture is dry, screw the lid on the jar. Apply more of the papier-mâché mixture to build up the sides of the boots and to add fullness to the bottom of the suit. Be careful to leave a little space between the two halves so they don't stick together as the mixture dries.

Add papier-mâché around the face area and downward, forming the beard. For the nose, roll a ball of papier-mâché. Form the bridge of the nose by pinching one side of the ball between your fingers; press it onto the face, blending the edges. For the cheeks, roll two smaller balls; press them onto the face, blending the edges. Add small pieces of papier-mâché to the face for the eyebrows. Form the mustache with two equal amounts of the papier-mâché mixture; press the mustache pieces onto the face, overlapping the top of the beard. Use the tip of a pointed tool to create the mouth.

Mold and shape the hat with the papier-mâché mixture. For the fur trim, roll a rope and press it around Santa's head, covering the bottom of the hat. Smooth the ends of the fur trim. Add a small ball to the tip of the hat for the pom-pom. Allow the figure to dry somewhat before adding more of the mixture.

For the arms, make a rope of papier-mâché. Curve and press the rope across the front of the body with an end on each side of the head about even with the eyebrows. Add mixture on the arms for the fur trim. For the belt, roll a long rope and press it around the waist (lid for the jar). For the belt buckle, roll a very thin rope and shape it into a rectangle at the center front of the belt. Carve around the inside area of the belt, creating a thin raised "prong" in the center.

For the fur trim on the bottom half of the suit, roll a long rope and a short rope. Press the long rope around the bottom edge of the suit and a short rope on the center front. Smooth the ends of the fur trim. Apply a smooth layer of the papier-mâché mixture to the bottom of the boots. Place the figure on a wire rack to dry.

PAINT THE SANTA

Use a flat brush to base-coat all surfaces of the figure IW; let dry. Apply a second coat of IW; let dry.

Paint the face AP. Use TA to paint the suit and hat. Use BG to paint all the fur trim, including the pom-pom at the tip of the hat. Paint the belt AM and the mittens TG. Use RU to paint the boots. Paint the belt buckle PG.

FINISH THE SANTA

When the paint is dry, spray the Santa with a coat of matte-finish spray; let dry. Cover all surfaces with antiquing medium. Immediately wipe off the excess medium with a paper towel, leaving more color in the recessed areas. Let the medium dry.

Use a liner brush to paint the eyes LI. Mix a little CR with AP; use the round brush and the mixture to blush the cheeks and nose.

When the paint is dry, lightly spray the Santa with a coat of matte-finish spray. Allow to dry and apply a second coat.

Drill a small hole on the inside of the arm. Trim the greenery into a tree shape and glue into the hole.

—*Designed by Kathy Cornell*

Little Lambs

Shown on page 114 and right.

YOU WILL NEED

For one lamb:

Tracing paper

Plush felt: One 18×22½" piece each of antique white and black

Matching sewing thread

Quilting thread: off-white and black

Polyester fiberfill

Dental-floss tape

Large-eye needle

2—5mm light-blue pom-poms

2 small black beads

Glue

24" length of 1½"-wide wire-edge ribbon

Small bell

INSTRUCTIONS

Trace the head, ear, and tail patterns *below right* onto tracing paper; cut them out. Sew all pieces with right sides together, using ⅛" seam allowances unless otherwise noted.

CUT THE FELT

From the antique-white plush felt, cut the tail and one 7¾×11¼" rectangle for the body. From the black plush felt, cut two heads, two ears, and four 3" squares for the legs.

SEW THE LAMB

Fold the body rectangle in half with right sides together to measure 5⅛×7¾". Sew together the long edges opposite the fold, forming a tube. Use off-white quilting thread to hand-sew running stitches around one open end of the tube. Pull the thread to tightly close the tail end of the tube; knot the thread securely. Turn the body right side out, and stuff it with polyester fiberfill.

Sew the head pieces together, leaving the top edge open. Turn the head right side out, and stuff it with fiberfill. Hand-sew running stitches

around the open neck edge of the body. Insert the head into the neck opening, with the body seam centered on the underside of the lamb's body. Adjust the stuffing, and pull the thread to gather the body snugly around the head; knot the thread securely.

Use black quilting thread to sew the head to the body and the ears to the head. Use off-white quilting thread to sew the tail to the body.

For the legs, tightly roll the 3" black felt squares into cylinders, and sew down the long edges. Sew the legs to the underside of the body,

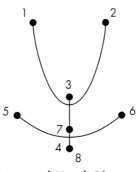

Nose and Mouth Diagram

adjusting their locations so the lamb will stand. Our lamb's legs are approximately 1" apart; the back pair is 2" behind the front pair.

ADD THE FACE

Thread the large-eye needle with dental-floss tape. Referring to the Nose and Mouth Diagram *above* and the head pattern for placement, stitch the nose and mouth. The needle comes up at the odd numbers and goes down at the even numbers.

For the eyes, glue light-blue pom-poms to the head; glue black beads to the pom-poms. Wrap the ribbon around the lamb's neck, and tie it into a bow. Trim the ribbon ends. Sew the bell to the ribbon.

—Designed by Karen Booth

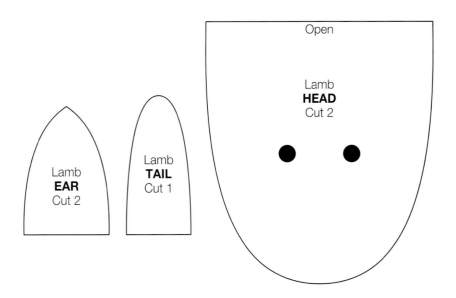

Lamb **EAR** Cut 2

Lamb **TAIL** Cut 1

Open

Lamb **HEAD** Cut 2

Good Pet Christmas Stockings

Shown on pages 115 and 128.

YOU WILL NEED

For each stocking:

Graph paper

Tracing paper

Tissue wrapping paper

Embroidery needle

Large-eye needle

#8 pearl cotton: green and yellow

10" length of ¼"-wide green grosgrain ribbon

For Good Dog Stocking:

Kunin Rainbow felt:

2—9x12" pieces of red

1—9x12" piece each of antique gold, antique white, black, cadet blue, cashmere tan, kelly green, and soft beige

Cotton embroidery floss: black, green, red, tan, and yellow

Sewing thread: black, blue, gold, green, tan, and white

For Good Cat Stocking:

Kunin Rainbow felt:

2—9x12" pieces of red

1—9x12" piece each of antique white, black, butterscotch, deep rose, kelly green, leaf green, and silver gray

Cotton embroidery floss: black, gray, green, pink, red, white, and yellow

Sewing thread: black, green, pink, and yellow

Light beige heavy rug thread for whiskers

INSTRUCTIONS

Enlarge the stocking pattern, *page 131,* on graph paper. Trace the appliqué patterns *(pages 129–130)* onto tracing paper. Cut out each pattern piece.

CUT THE FELT

Good Dog Stocking:

From the red felt, cut:

• 2 stockings and 1 heart

From the antique gold felt, cut:

• 1 star, 1 doghouse base, and 1 ball stripe

From the antique white felt, cut:

• 1 of each dog body and 1 pair of legs

From the black felt, cut:

• 1 doorway, 1 of each spot, and 2 noses

From the cadet blue felt, cut:

• 1 doghouse and 1 ball stripe

From the cashmere tan felt, cut:

• 1 large bone cuff, 2 bones, 1 of each dog face, 1 of each ear, and 1 spot

From the kelly green felt, cut:

• 1 doghouse roof and 1 ball

From the soft beige felt, cut:

• 1 small bone cuff

Good Cat Stocking:

From the red felt, cut:

• 2 stockings

From the antique white felt, cut:

• 1 pair of legs, 1 face, and 1 hat band

From the black felt, cut:

• 1 cat body with tail

From the butterscotch felt, cut:

• 1 cat body, 1 of each paw, and 1 hat

From the deep rose felt, cut:

• 1 large heart, 2 small hearts, 2 heart noses, and 2 inner ears

From the kelly green felt, cut:

• 1 large fish cuff and 1 yarn ball

From the leaf green felt, cut:

• 1 small fish cuff and 1 box

From the silver gray, cut:

• 1 mouse and 1 mouse ear

EMBROIDER THE LETTERING

To personalize the stocking, practice writing the desired name on scrap paper to fit in the small bone cuff or small fish cuff. When you are pleased with the name, trace it onto the tissue wrapping paper.

Pin the tissue pattern in place on the small cuff shape. Use four plies of red floss to work backstitches and French knots over the pencil lines, stitching through the tissue pattern and felt. When the embroidery is finished, carefully tear away the tissue wrapping paper.

Trace "Woof" or "Meow" onto the tissue wrapping paper and use one strand of green pearl cotton to straight-stitch and backstitch the lettering on the star or the large heart.

MAKE THE TWISTED CORDING

Follow these directions to make twisted cording in the colors indicated in the appliqué instructions *below* for each stocking. For the dogs' and cats' collars and the mouse's tail, cut a 36" length of floss and use three plies. For the thin ball strip, cut a 15" length of floss and use three plies. Cut a 110" length of green floss and use all six plies to make twisted cord for the yarn.

Knot one end of the plies together. Thread a large-eye needle with the plies of floss. Secure the knot to a stationary object and twist the opposite end until the floss is very tightly twisted and begins to kink. Holding the ends, fold the floss in half with the needle at the fold ; the two halves will twist around each other. Knot the end opposite the fold to secure it.

APPLIQUÉ THE STOCKING

Refer to the photographs, *pages 115 and 128,* to arrange the felt pieces and as a guide for embroidery. Use one ply of matching sewing thread to whipstitch. Use two plies of floss for

Continued

running stitches, straight stitches, backstitches, and cross-stitches, unless otherwise specified. Use six plies of floss to make French-knot eyes, and four plies of floss for all other French knots. Blanket-stitch with one strand of pearl cotton or three plies of floss. Use one ply of matching floss to couch the twisted cording.

DOG STOCKING

Use tan floss to blanket-stitch around the large bone cuff. Center the personalized small bone on the large bone and place at the top of the stocking. Work green running stitches through all layers, sewing ⅛" from the edges of the small bone.

Place the doorway behind the opening in the doghouse. Use yellow pearl cotton to make running stitches ⅛" from the edge of the opening. Sew the heart above the doorway with green French knots. Make red cross-stitches across the doghouse base. Arrange the doghouse, roof, and base on the stocking. Whip-stitch the pieces in place. Use yellow pearl cotton to blanket-stitch along the bottom edge of the roof.

Whipstitch the face, ears, spots, legs, and nose on each dog's body. Whipstitch the dogs to the stocking front, tacking down the ears of the sitting dog. Make black French knots. Straight-stitch the mouth and paw lines black. Use tan to backstitch the chin line on the sitting dog. Make yellow and green twisted cording for the collars as described on *page 127*. Insert the needle from front to back at one edge of the neck, go under the neck, and bring the needle to the front at the opposite edge of the neck. Tie the cording into a bow around the neck. Tie a knot in the cording tails about 1" from the bow; trim the cording below the knots. Couch the twisted cording in place.

For the ball, make red cross-stitches across the antique gold stripe and yellow French knots across the cadet blue stripe. Position the stripes on the ball. Make running stitches ¹⁄₁₆" from the edges of the stripes, using green floss for the gold stripe and red floss for the blue stripe. Sew the ball to the stocking with green running stitches ⅛" from the edge. Make red twisted cording for the thin stripe as described on *page 127*. Insert the needle from back to front at one edge of the ball, go over the ball, and bring the needle to the back at the opposite edge of the ball; knot. Couch the cording in place.

Arrange the bones on the stocking front. Sew the bones to the stocking front with tan floss and running stitches ⅛" from the edges. Use one strand of green pearl cotton to sew the "Woof" star to the stocking front, alternating straight stitches with French knots.

CAT STOCKING

Use yellow pearl cotton to blanket-stitch around the large fish cuff. Center the personalized small fish on the large fish and place at the top of the stocking. Work green running stitches through all layers, sewing ⅛" from the edges of the small fish.

Whipstitch the heart nose and inner ears on the cat-in-the-box. Arrange all the felt pieces for the cat-in-the-box on the stocking front. Use green floss to make running stitches a scant ¹⁄₁₆" from the edges of the box and to backstitch the inner box lines. Whipstitch the cat and the paws in place. Make black French knots. Straight-stitch the mouth, eyebrow, and paw lines black. Use yellow pearl cotton to backstitch the chin and ear lines. Make red twisted cording for the collar as described on *page 127*. Insert the needle from front to back at one edge of the neck, go

Continued

**DOG STOCKING
PATTERN PIECES**
Cut 1 each

CAT STOCKING PATTERN PIECES
Cut 1 each

MeoW

under the neck, and bring the needle to the front at the opposite edge of the neck. Tie the cording into a bow around the neck. Tie a knot in the cording tails about 1" from the bow; trim the cording below the knots. Couch the twisted cording in place. For the whiskers, use light beige heavy rug thread to make a single turkey stitch on each side of the mouth.

For the sitting cat, use black to backstitch the line separating the legs. Place the legs and face on the cat's body. Make black running stitches ⅛" from the edges of the face and from the top edge of the legs. Whipstitch the heart nose to the face. Arrange all the pieces for the sitting cat on the stocking front. Whipstitch the cat's body and tail to the stocking. Make French knots, using green for the eyes and black for the mouth. Use black to straight-stitch the mouth and paw lines. Straight-stitch the eyebrows white. Use yellow pearl cotton to make running stitches ¹⁄₁₆" from the edges of the hat and to backstitch the fold line. Sew the hat band in place with red running stitches ¹⁄₁₆" from the edges. Use yellow twisted cording for the collar and rug thread for the whiskers as described for the cat-in-the-box.

Place the mouse on the stocking front and use pink to sew running stitches ⅛" from the edges. Use pink to straight-stitch the ear in place. Make black French knots. Use rug thread to make turkey stitches for the whiskers. Make gray twisted cording for the tail as described on *page 127*. Insert the needle through the tail end of the mouse from back to front and drape the cording on the stocking front. Tie a knot about ½" from the desired end of the tail; trim the excess cording ½" below the knot. Couch the twisted cording in place.

Whipstitch the yarn ball to the stocking front. Make green twisted cording for the yarn as described on *page 127*, using six plies of floss. Insert the needle from back to front at

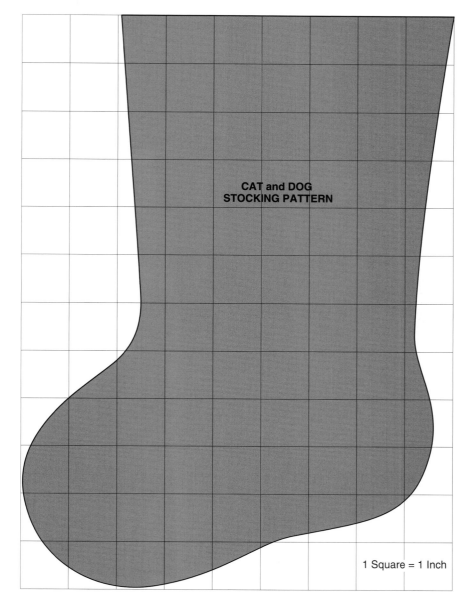

CAT and DOG STOCKING PATTERN

1 Square = 1 Inch

one edge of the ball near the bottom, wrap the cording over the ball, and bring the needle to the back at the opposite edge of the ball. Continue wrapping the cording around the bottom three-fourths of the ball. Then wrap the cording around the top one-fourth of the ball in the opposite direction. For the yarn tail, drape the cording on the stocking front. Tie a knot about ½" from the desired end; trim the excess cording ½" below the knot. Couch the twisted cording to the ball and to the stocking front.

Arrange the large "Meow" heart and small hearts on the stocking front, positioning the large heart over the yarn tail. Sew the hearts to the

stocking front with yellow and red French knots. Thread a needle with six plies of green floss and tie a knot about ½" from one end. Insert the needle through the center on one small heart with the knot on the front; knot again on the back.

FINISH THE STOCKING
Center the stocking front on the stocking back; pin together. Use yellow pearl cotton to blanket-stitch the stocking front to the stocking back, leaving the top edge open.

For the hanging loop, fold the ¼"-wide green ribbon in half. Sew the ends to the top inside corner on the heel side of the stocking.
—*Designed by Robin Kingsley*

Wire and Bead Candleholder

Shown on page 116 and below.

YOU WILL NEED

4 small glass containers

Artistic Wire Ltd. permanent colored copper wire: natural 24-gauge, green 16-gauge, and purple 26-gauge

Wire cutters

Assorted glass beads

4 taper candles

INSTRUCTIONS

Wrap the natural wire 8 to 10 times around the four containers half-way between the base and the neck. Repeat at the neck of the containers. Use the green wire to loosely weave the two natural wraps together, bending the green wire around the wraps and shaping it as desired. Attach the beads and create a "spider-web" with the purple wire, wrapping it between the natural and green wires and around itself.

—*Designed by Nancy Wyatt*

Painted Stemware

Shown on page 117.

YOU WILL NEED

Clear glass wineglasses

Liquitex Glossies high gloss acrylic enamel: black, blue purple, bright blue, green, red, white, and yellow

Assorted paintbrushes, including flat and liner

INSTRUCTIONS

Wash and dry the glasses. Paint a white circle on the glass for the ball ornament. When the paint is dry, use green, red, blue purple, and yellow to paint zigzag stripes across the ball, varying the widths and spacing. To add dots, use the handle end of a paintbrush. For the hanger, paint thin black and white overlapping lines. Personalize the glasses with green. Let the paint dry. To heat-set, place glasses in a cold oven in a well-ventilated area and then bake for 30-40 minutes at 325°. Cool on a cookie sheet.

—*Designed by Nancy Wyatt*

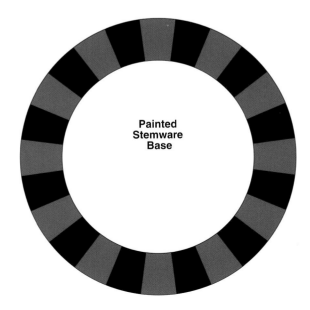

Painted Stemware Base

Hanky Envelope

Shown on page 121.

YOU WILL NEED

Purchased handkerchief
Matching sewing thread
⅝"-diameter button
Bead

INSTRUCTIONS

For the sides of the envelope, fold opposite corners of the handkerchief to the center, overlapping the points slightly; press. Fold up a third corner of the handkerchief to overlap about ⅛" of the first two folded sections, forming the bottom of the envelope; press. Hand-sew the overlapping edges together with a small running stitch. For the flap, fold down the remaining corner and sew the button and bead to the point.

—Designed by Nancy Wyatt

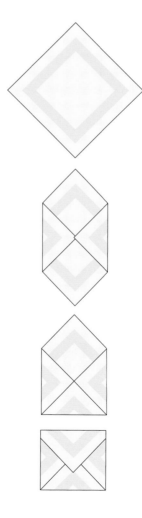

Hanky Pincushion

Shown on page 118.

YOU WILL NEED

Purchased square handkerchief
Matching cotton fabric
Matching sewing thread
Polyester fiberfill

INSTRUCTIONS

Measure the center of the handkerchief to determine the desired finished size of the cushion; add ½" seam allowances. Use these measurements to cut 2 squares from the cotton fabric.

Center one square, right side down, on the wrong side of the handkerchief. Sew the square to the handkerchief ½" from the edges of the square. Fold all edges of the handkerchief toward the center. With right sides facing, pin the squares together with the handkerchief in between, being careful that the handkerchief does not extend into the ½" seam allowance. Sew the squares together a scant ½" from the edges, leaving an opening on one side for turning. Trim the seams, clip the corners, and turn right side out. Press. Stuff the cushion firmly with polyester fiberfill and slip-stitch the opening closed.

—Designed by Nancy Wyatt

Bath Mitt

Shown on page 120.

YOU WILL NEED

13" square purchased face cloth
Matching sewing thread

INSTRUCTIONS

To make the pocket, fold up 4" to the front of the face cloth and baste the short edges of the pocket in place. Fold the cloth in half with the pocket on the inside and sew the long edges together, creating a tube. Refold the cloth, centering the seam. Sew together the short edges opposite the pocket. Turn the mitt right side out.

—Designed by Nancy Wyatt

Pressed Flower Soaps

Shown on page 120.

YOU WILL NEED

Delta Melt & Pour Glycerine Soap:
    Crystal Clear
Delta Fragrant Accents: scent of
    your choice
Microwave-safe bowl
Delta No-Tip Soap Molds:
    Rectangles & Squares, Ovals
    & Circles
Pressed flowers
OR YOU WILL NEED
Block of transparent glycerine soap
Microwave-safe bowl
Fragrance of your choice
Rectangle and oval molds
Pressed flowers

INSTRUCTIONS

Cut the block of glycerine soap into pieces and melt in a bowl in a microwave oven, following the manufacturer's directions. Add the fragrance of your choice and mix well. Pour about a ¼"-thick layer of soap into the mold. Arrange the pressed flowers facedown on the soap in the mold. Carefully pour more soap to fill the mold, covering the flowers. Let the soap harden. Turn the mold upside down and gently tap the underside of the mold to release the soap.

—Designed by Nancy Wyatt

Holiday Blessings Sampler

Shown on page 119.

YOU WILL NEED

18×14" piece of 32-count ivory linen

Cotton embroidery floss in the colors listed in the key *below*

Mill Hill seed beads in the colors listed in the key below

Needle

Needlework frame

Desired mat and frame

INSTRUCTIONS

Zigzag stitch or overcast the edges of the fabric to prevent fraying. Center and stitch the sampler on the linen. Use two plies (2X) of floss to work the stitches over two threads unless otherwise specified in the key. Work the remaining stitches over the number of threads indicated on the chart and referring to the diagrams below. For the Algerian eyelets, give each stitch a gentle tug to open a small hole in the center. Attach the seed beads using one ply of matching floss. Press the stitchery facedown on a soft towel. Mat and frame the piece as desired.

—Designed by Robin Kingsley

Anchor		DMC	
212	◆	561	Dark seafoam
210	◩	562	Medium seafoam
208	✕	563	True seafoam
874	•	676	Light old gold
885	—	677	Pale old gold
891	✳	729	Medium old gold
169	■	806	Dark peacock blue
167	○	3766	Light peacock blue
1006	▲	3831	Dark raspberry
028	✚	3832	Medium raspberry
031	╱	3833	Light raspberry

BACKSTITCH

212	╱	561	Dark seafoam – leaves and tendrils top and row 18
1066	╱	3765	Deep peacock blue – lettering top and row 14

ALGERIAN EYELET (1X)

885	✳	677	Pale old gold – row 2

FRENCH KNOT (1X wrapped twice)

1066	●	3765	Deep peacock blue – lettering top and row 14

HERRINGBONE STITCH (2X)

028	✕✕	3832	Medium raspberry – row 18

LAZY DAISY (2X)

210	⬭	562	Medium seafoam – row 16

LONG-ARM CROSS-STITCH (1X)

210	✖	562	Medium seafoam – row 14

QUEEN STITCH (1X)

167	◈	3766	Light peacock blue – row 5

RICE STITCH (1X)

1006	◇	3831	Dark raspberry and
031	✕	3833	Light raspberry – row 15

STRAIGHT STITCH (1X)

212	╱	561	Dark seafoam – flowers row 16

MILL HILL BEADS

	✕	02013	Red red – holly berries top and rows 16 and 18
	✕	02011	Victorian gold – top and rows 2, 4, 11, and 18

Stitch count: *139 high x 70 wide*

Finished design sizes:
32-count fabric – 8⅝ x 4⅓ inches
28-count fabric – 10 x 5 inches
36-count fabric – 7¾ x 3⅞ inches

Algerian Eyelet

French Knot

Herringbone Stitch

Laisy Daisy

Long-Arm Cross-Stitch

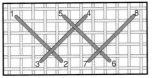

Queen Stitch

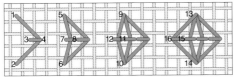

Rice Stitch

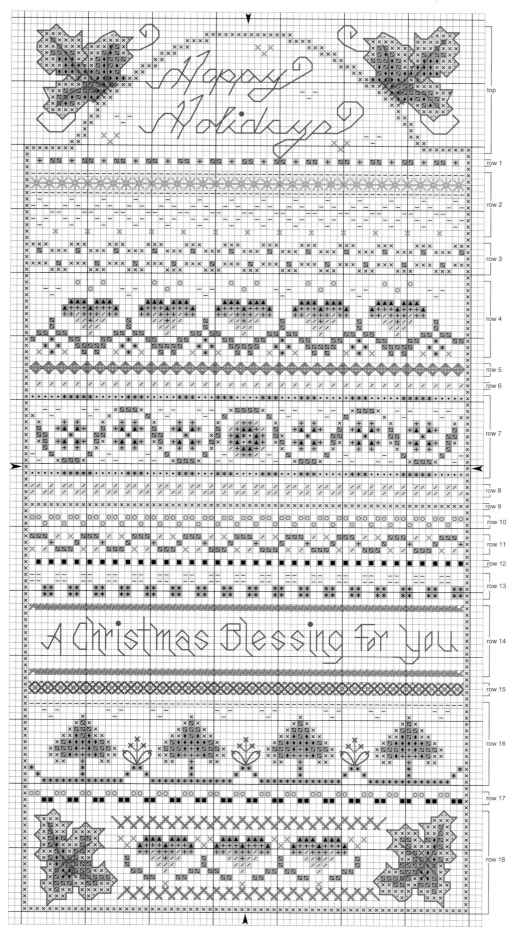

Velvet Stocking with Crocheted Snowflake Cuff

Shown on page 122.

YOU WILL NEED

For the Stocking:

Graph paper

¾ yard of white velvet

¾ yard of lightweight white lining fabric

Matching sewing thread

½ yard of ⅛"-diameter cording

9" length of 1"-wide ivory satin ribbon

5½"-wide piece of lace (see the Crocheted Snowflake Cuff, left)

For the Cuff:

1 ball DMC Size 40 Ecru Cordonnet thread

Size 13 steel crochet hook

Gauge: 6 ch-2 sps = 1"; 1 pattern repeat (22 rows) = 4"

ABBREVIATIONS

Beg	beginning
Bl	block
Ch	chain
Dc	double crochet
Dec	decrease
Inc	increase
Rep	repeat
RS	right side
Sc	single crochet
Sl	slip
Sk	skip
Sp	space
St(s)	stitch(es)
Trc	triple crochet
Yo	yarn over

STITCHES

Block	3 dc
Space	ch 2, dc
Triple crochet	yo twice, insert hook into designated place, pull up loop; [yo and through 2 loops] 3 times

INSTRUCTIONS

Enlarge the stocking pattern, *opposite,* on graph paper. Add ½" seam allowances beyond the drawn lines and cut out the completed pattern piece. Sew all pieces with right sides together using ½" seam allowances, unless otherwise noted.

Use the stocking pattern to cut two pieces from velvet and two from the lining fabric.

Machine-baste the lining shapes to the wrong side of the velvet stocking front and the stocking back. Sew the stocking front to the back, leaving the top edge open. Trim the seams, and clip the curves. Turn the stocking right side out.

Zigzag-stitch or overcast the top edge of the stocking. For the piping, turn under ¾" at the top of the stocking and place the cording inside and up against the fold. Use a zipper foot to sew through all fabric layers close to the cording.

For the hanging loop, fold the ribbon in half. Tuck the loop ends under the folded fabric at the top corner on the heel side of the stocking. Then hand-sew the loop in place.

Slip the cuff over the stocking so the top edge is just below the piping. Hand-sew the top edge of the cuff, *right,* to the stocking.

CROCHET THE CUFF

Ch 61 loosely. Turn at end of each row throughout.

Row 1: (RS) Dc in 4th ch from hook and next 6 ch; [ch 2, sk 2 ch, dc in next ch—foundation space made; dc in next 3 ch—foundation block made] 3 times; [ch 2, sk 2 ch, dc in next ch] 5 times; dc in next 3 ch; [ch 2, sk 2 ch, dc in next ch] 4 times; dc in last 3 ch—58 sts; turn.

Row 2: Ch 5, dc in 4th ch from hook and next ch—beg inc bl made; dc in dc; ch 2, sk 2 dc, dc in dc—Sp over Bl made; [ch 2, sk ch 2 sp, dc in dc—sp over sp made] 2 times; [2 dc in ch-2 sp, dc in dc—bl over sp made]; sp over sp; dc in 3 dc—bl over bl made; sp over sp; block over sp; [sp over sp] 3 times; [sp over bl, bl over sp] 3 times; dc in next 6 dc, dc in top of turning ch.

Row 3: Ch 3, dc in 6 dc; sp over bl; sp over sp, sp over bl; bl over sp; sp over bl; [sp over sp] 4 times; [bl over sp; sp over bl] 2 times; [sp over sp] 3 times; sp over bl; [trc in top of turning st; trc in base of previous trc]—ending inc bl made.

Row 4-11: Follow chart, inc at beg or end of each row as indicated.

Row 12: Sl st across 3 sts of ending inc block—beg dec bl made; Ch 3 (counts as dc), dc in dc; 2 dc in ch 2

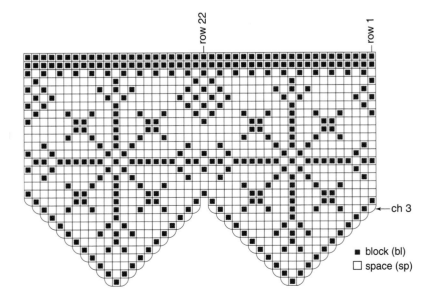

■ block (bl)
□ space (sp)

sp, dc in dc;—bl over sp made; follow chart across row as established.

Row 13: Follow chart across to last open space; work [bl over sp]; leave last 3 sts unworked—ending dec bl made; turn.

Row 14: Rep Row 12.

Row 15-22: Follow chart, dec at beg or end of each row as indicated. Rep rows 1–22 three times or until desired length.

Edging. Working in end of rows, attach thread at outside edge of finished end. Ch 1, sc in end st; [ch 3, sc in end st of next row] across. Finish off. Press lightly. Stiffen as desired.

—Designed by Nancy Wyatt

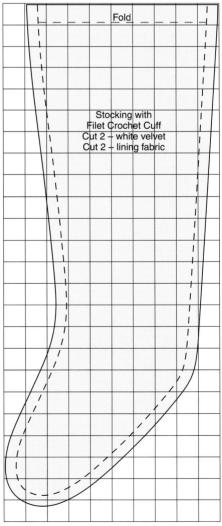

Fold

Stocking with
Filet Crochet Cuff
Cut 2 – white velvet
Cut 2 – lining fabric

1 Square = 1 Inch

Painted Dragonfly Sachet

Shown on page 123.

YOU WILL NEED

2—6" square purchased fabric coasters
Denami Design dragonfly rubber stamp
Deka Permanent fabric paint: Black, Cactus Green, Colorless Extender, Santa Fe Aqua, and Violet
Paintbrush
1 yard of ⅜"-wide hand-dyed bias-cut silk ribbon
Large-eye needle
Polyester fiberfill or dried lavender buds or other filling

INSTRUCTIONS

Ink the stamp with black and apply it to the center of one coaster. Let the paint dry.

Mix Colorless Extender with Cactus Green, Santa Fe Aqua, and Violet to achieve the desired colors. Use a paintbrush and the lightened paints to color in the dragonfly. When the paint is dry, heat-set with an iron on the wrong side for 1 minute at the highest setting or for 2 minutes at medium setting.

Cut the silk ribbon in half. Thread the large-eye needle with one ribbon length. With wrong sides facing, sew the coasters together along three edges by weaving the ribbon through the eyelets; do not cut ribbon. Fill the sachet with dried lavender, then close the remaining edge of the sachet with the ribbon. To hide the ribbon ends, use the needle to pull them to the inside of the sachet. Thread the remaining ribbon length through the eyelets at the bottom corner of the sachet. Tie the ribbon in a bow and cut the ends at an angle.

—Designed by Nancy Wyatt

Rose Sachet

Shown on page 123.

YOU WILL NEED

2—6" square purchased fabric coasters
1 yard of 2"-wide wire-edge ribbon
3—2"-long silk rose leaves
3—¾"- to 1¼"-diameter purchased ribbon flowers
Assorted glass beads
1 yard of ⅜"-wide hand-dyed bias-cut silk ribbon
Large-eyed needle
Polyester fiberfill or dried lavender buds or other filling

INSTRUCTIONS

To make the rose, pull on the wire at the bottom edge of the ribbon to gather the rose. Sew the rose together at the bottom to hold the shape; trim off the excess wire. Arrange the large rose, leaves, and flowers on the front of one coaster and sew in place. Sew the beads to the coaster, filling in any gaps between the flowers.

Thread the large-eye needle with the ¼"-wide silk ribbon. With wrong sides facing, sew the coasters together along three edges by weaving the ribbon through the eyelets; do not cut ribbon. Fill the sachet with dried lavender, then close the remaining edge of the sachet with the ribbon. Tie the ribbon in a bow and cut the ends at an angle.

—Designed by Nancy Wyatt

Rose

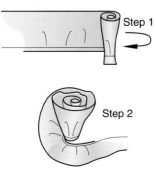

Step 1

Step 2

A Slice of Christmas Spice

Whether you host large holiday gatherings or small informal brunches, food takes center stage. Sweet Pepper Bruschetta (opposite) combines creamy texture with flavorful crunch. White chèvre cheese, sweet red peppers, and pesto will become a festive Mediterranean addition to your holiday table. Swirls of red and green Lahvosh slices (below) are so easy to prepare—it's the perfect make-ahead choice for parties. Recipes begin on page 145.

You might be tempted to serve this cheesy pie (opposite) as a luncheon main course because it's so rich; it also makes a satisfying appetizer. Roasted red peppers and chèvre cheese are baked together into a slice of heaven on a crust. Make it in a quiche dish or mini-muffin pans for bite-size appetizers.

Keep a good thing going. That's how you'll feel about the cheese molds shown above. All begin with cream cheese flavored with onions and garlic. Mold each with one of three fillings—walnut and gorgonzola, roasted red pepper, or pesto—to create variations on a theme. Each one is as good as the other.

hat's for dessert? The most-asked question at holiday dinners can be answered with this fresh and colorful delicacy. Raspberry White Chocolate Brownies (above) marry the tart flavor of red raspberries with the creamy perfection of white chocolate. Cut into star shapes for fun, these brownies make great gifts as well as a luscious dessert. Serve them with steaming cups of Cinnamon Hot Chocolate (above). Topped with frothy whipped cream and chocolate shavings, this sweet drink will warm you from the inside out.

A little dessert with your coffee? Or is it the other way around? Either way, everyone will rave about the layered flavors of chocolate and coffee in these cappuccino brownies (above). Cut into neat squares, this mocha dessert presents a delicious dessert that's as pretty and welcome as a holiday package.

Key West meets Italy for the holidays! Lime-pistachio cookies (above) are finger food for every sweet tooth in the holiday crowd. The colorful dessert cookies blend the hues of the season tastefully. Crispy lime cookies, stuffed with creamy lime-pistachio filling, are cool and sweetly tart for a refreshing dessert treat.

Lime Sandwich Cookies

Shown on page 144.

Tip: To help keep the rolls of dough from flattening on the refrigerator shelf, place them in tall drinking glasses.

YOU WILL NEED

1   cup butter (no substitutes)
1   cup sugar
½   teaspoon baking powder
1   egg
1   teaspoon finely shredded lime peel (set aside)
2   tablespoons lime juice
3   cups all-purpose flour
    Several drops green food coloring
    Lime-Pistachio Filling

INSTRUCTIONS

Beat butter in a mixing bowl with an electric mixer on medium to high speed for 30 seconds. Add sugar and baking powder; beat until combined. Beat in egg and lime juice until combined. Beat in as much of the flour as you can with the mixer. Stir in lime peel and any remaining flour with a wooden spoon. Tint the dough the desired color with green food coloring.

Shape dough into two 8"-long logs. Wrap in clear plastic wrap and twist ends tightly to seal. Chill dough for 4 to 24 hours.

Cut dough into ⅛"-thick slices; place slices 1" apart on an ungreased cookie sheet. Bake in a 375° oven for 7 to 8 minutes or until bottoms are lightly browned. Transfer cookies to wire racks to cool. Spread bottom surface of half of the cookies with about 1 tablespoon of the Lime-Pistachio Filling. Top with another cookie right side up. **Makes 40 sandwich cookies.**

Lime-Pistachio Filling. Beat ¼ cup butter (no substitutes) in a mixing bowl with an electric mixer on medium to high speed about 30 seconds or until softened. Gradually beat in 1⅓ cups sifted powdered sugar. Beat in 3 tablespoons lime juice until smooth. Gradually beat in enough sifted powdered sugar (1⅓ to 2 cups) to make of spreading consistency. Stir in ⅓ cup finely chopped pistachio nuts.

Lahvosh Slices

Shown on page 138.

YOU WILL NEED

1   15" sesame seed lahvosh (Armenian cracker bread)
4   ounces soft-style cream cheese with chives and onion
¼   cup chopped, drained, marinated artichoke hearts
2   tablespoons diced pimiento
1   teaspoon dried oregano, crushed
6   ounces thinly sliced prosciutto or cooked ham
4   ounces sliced provolone cheese
2   large romaine lettuce leaves, ribs removed

INSTRUCTIONS

Soften lahvosh by holding each side briefly under gently running cold water. Place lahvosh, sesame side down, between two damp, clean, kitchen towels. Let stand about 1 hour or until pliable.

Stir together cream cheese, artichoke hearts, pimiento, and oregano. Remove top towel from lahvosh. Spread lahvosh with cream cheese mixture to edges. Arrange prosciutto or ham over cream cheese layer. Arrange cheese slices in the center. Place lettuce leaves along one edge of cheese slices.

Roll from lettuce edge, using the towel to lift and roll the bread. Cover and chill, seam side down, for 2 to 24 hours. Trim ends of roll; cut into 1"-thick slices. **Makes 14 slices.**

Raspberry and White Chocolate Brownies

Shown on page 142.

YOU WILL NEED

½   cup butter (no substitutes)
2   ounces white chocolate baking bar or squares, cut up
2   eggs
⅔   cup sugar
1   teaspoon vanilla
1   cup all-purpose flour
½   cup chopped toasted almonds
½   teaspoon baking powder
    Dash salt
1   cup fresh raspberries
2   ounces white chocolate baking bar or squares, melted

INSTRUCTIONS

Line an 8×8×2" baking pan with foil. Grease foil; set pan aside.

Melt butter and cut-up white chocolate in a medium saucepan over low heat, stirring frequently; remove from heat. Stir in eggs, sugar, and vanilla. Beat lightly with a wooden spoon just until combined. Stir in flour, almonds, baking powder, and salt.

Spread batter in the prepared pan. Sprinkle with raspberries. Bake in a 350° oven for 30 to 35 minutes or until golden. Cool in pan on a wire rack. Remove from pan by lifting foil. Cut with any shape cookie cutter or cut into bars. Drizzle cutouts or bars with melted white chocolate.

Makes 20 bars.

Roasted Red Pepper and Chèvre Appetizer Cheesecake

Shown on page 140.

YOU WILL NEED

- 1 **cup crushed crisp sesame breadsticks**
- 2 **tablespoons butter or margarine, melted**
- 1 **7-ounce jar roasted red peppers, well drained**
- 8 **ounces goat cheese (chèvre), broken up**
- 1 **cup ricotta cheese**
- ½ **cup whipping cream**
- 2 **eggs**
- 2 **tablespoons all-purpose flour**
- 1 **clove garlic, quartered**
- 1 **teaspoon snipped fresh thyme or ¼ teaspoon dried thyme, crushed**
- 1 **teaspoon snipped fresh rosemary or ⅛ teaspoon dried rosemary, crushed**
  Assorted crackers
  Fresh herbs (optional)

INSTRUCTIONS

For crust, combine crushed breadsticks and melted butter or margarine in a mixing bowl. Press mixture evenly on the bottom and about 1" up the sides of an 8" springform pan; set aside.

For filling, chop ½ cup drained peppers; set aside. Place remaining peppers, goat cheese, and ricotta cheese in blender container or food processor bowl. Cover and blend or process for 1 to 1½ minutes or until smooth. Add whipping cream, eggs, flour, garlic, thyme, and rosemary. Cover and blend or process for 1 to 1½ minutes more or until smooth. Stir in chopped pepper.

Pour filling into crust-lined springform pan. Place the springform pan on a shallow baking pan on the oven rack. Bake in a 350° oven for 35 to 40 minutes or until center appears nearly set when shaken.

Remove springform pan from baking pan. Cool on a wire rack for 15 minutes. Use a narrow metal spatula to loosen crust from sides of pan. Cool 30 minutes more. Remove sides of the pan. Cool for 1 hour; cover and chill at least 3 hours. Let cheesecake stand at room temperature for 30 minutes before serving. Garnish with fresh herbs, if desired. Serve with assorted crackers. **Makes 12 to 16 appetizer servings.**

Three-Way Cheese Molds

Shown on page 141.

YOU WILL NEED

- 2 **8-ounce packages cream cheese, softened**
- ⅓ **cup dairy sour cream**
- ¼ **cup finely chopped onion**
- 1 **large clove garlic, minced**
  Assorted crackers
  Pine nuts, walnuts, cilantro or basil for garnish

INSTRUCTIONS

Beat cream cheese and sour cream in a large mixing bowl until smooth. Stir in onion and garlic. Divide mixture into three equal portions. Divide mixture into three equal portions, about ¾ cup each. Line three latté cups or three 6- to 10-ounce custard cups or molds with plastic wrap.

Gorgonzola-Walnut Mold. To one portion add ⅓ cup crumbled Gorgonzola or other blue cheese (1½ ounces). Spoon half of the mixture into a lined cup. Sprinkle with ¼ cup finely chopped toasted walnuts. Top with remaining chese mixture. Cover; refrigerate up to 24 hours.

Roasted Pepper Mold. To second portion add 2 tablespoons snipped fresh cilantro, dash ground red pepper, and dash ground cumin. Spoon half of this mixture into a lined up. Top with ¼ cup canned, drained, roasted red pepper. Spoon remaining cilantro

mixture on top of the pepper. Cover and refrigerate up to 24 hours.

Pesto Mold. Stir ⅛ cup purchased refrigerated pesto into remaining portion. Spoon half into remaining lined cup. Top with ⅛ cup pesto and 2 tablespoons chopped pine nuts. Cover with remaining pesto cheese mixture. Cover and refrigerate up to 24 hours.

To serve, unmold cheeses. Arrange on a platter and serve with crackers. Garnish with nuts, cilantro, chopped red peppers, or basil. **Makes 36 servings, 12 servings each.**

Cinnamon Hot Chocolate

Shown on page 142 and opposite.

YOU WILL NEED

- 3 **ounces semisweet chocolate**
- 1 **tablespoon sugar**
- ½ **to 1 teaspoon ground cinnamon**
- 2 **cups milk**
- ½ **teaspoon vanilla**
  Few drops of almond extract
  Whipped cream (optional)
  Chocolate shavings (optional)

INSTRUCTIONS

Cut chocolate into pieces; place in blender container or food processor bowl. Add sugar and cinnamon. Cover and blend or process until finely ground.

Cook and stir chocolate mixture and milk in a large saucepan over low heat about 10 minutes or until chocolate melts. Remove saucepan from heat; stir in vanilla and almond extract. Beat with a rotary beater until very frothy.

Serve in mugs. Top with whipped cream and chocolate shavings, if desired. **Makes about 4 (8-ounce) servings.**

Cappuccino Brownies

Shown on page 143.

YOU WILL NEED

½	cup butter or margarine
3	ounces unsweetened chocolate, cut up
1	cup granulated sugar
2	eggs
1	teaspoon vanilla
⅔	cup all-purpose flour
¼	teaspoon baking soda
1	teaspoon instant coffee crystals
1	tablespoon whipping cream
1	cup sifted powdered sugar
2	tablespoons butter or margarine
	Chocolate Frosting

INSTRUCTIONS

Melt the ½ cup butter or margarine and unsweetened chocolate in a medium saucepan over low heat, stirring constantly. Remove from heat; cool slightly. Stir in granulated sugar. Add eggs, one at a time, beating with a wooden spoon just until combined. Stir in vanilla.

Stir together flour and baking soda in a small bowl. Add flour mixture to chocolate mixture and stir just until combined. Spread batter in a greased 8×8×2" baking pan. Bake in a 350° oven for 30 minutes.

Meanwhile, for topping, dissolve coffee crystals in whipping cream. Beat together powdered sugar and the 2 tablespoons butter or margarine in a small mixing bowl with an electric mixer on medium speed. Add whipping cream mixture and beat until creamy. If necessary, add a little additional whipping cream until mixture is of spreading consistency. Spread over the warm brownies. Chill about 1 hour or until topping is set. Carefully spread Chocolate Frosting over brownies. Chill until frosting is set. Cut into bars. **Makes 16 bars.**

Chocolate Frosting. Combine 1 cup semisweet chocolate pieces and ⅓ cup whipping cream in small pan. Stir over low heat until chocolate is melted and mixture begins to thicken.

Sweet Pepper Bruschetta

Shown on page 139.

YOU WILL NEED

8	bias-cut slices (about ¾" thick) Italian country bread or crusty sourdough bread
½	cup soft goat cheese (chèvre) or other spreadable soft white cheese
¼	cup purchased basil pesto
1	7-ounce jar roasted red peppers, drained and cut into ½"-wide strips
	Snipped fresh herbs, such as basil, oregano, or thyme

INSTRUCTIONS

Toast or grill bread slices and spread each with soft cheese. Spread pesto atop cheese and top with pepper strips. Garnish with snipped herbs. Serve immediately. **Makes 8.**

Savory Nuts

Shown on page 139.

YOU WILL NEED

2	tablespoons white wine Worcestershire sauce
1	tablespoon olive oil
2	teaspoons snipped fresh thyme or ½ teaspoon dried thyme, crushed
1	teaspoon snipped fresh rosemary or ¼ teaspoon dried rosemary, crushed
¼	teaspoon salt
⅛	teaspoon ground red pepper
2	cups macadamia nuts, broken walnuts, and/or unblanched almonds

INSTRUCTIONS

Combine Worcestershire sauce, olive oil, thyme, rosemary, salt, and ground red pepper. Spread nuts in a 13×9×2" baking pan. Drizzle with oil mixture. Toss gently. Bake in a 350° oven for 12 to 15 minutes or until nuts are toasted, stirring occasionally. Spread on a large sheet of foil; cool. Store in an airtight container. **Makes 2 cups.**

Foods for Living

The gifts that you prepare in your kitchen may be the most welcome of all holiday offerings. Made to be consumed later, these culinary creations will be savored long after the holidays. Give the gift of a Tuscan trattoria with a basket filled with savory Italian goodies (opposite). Arrange fettuccine, aged Parmesan cheese, plump garlic bulbs, fragrant olive oil, bread-dipping sauce, and packets of such Mediterranean favorites as pine nuts and sun-dried tomatoes in the basket to fill your friends with la dolce vita. Wrap a jar of ready-to-cook Italian Herb and Dried Tomato Risotto in a colorful table napkin to add to the basket. Recipes begin on page 154.

Baby it's cold outside! And the best remedy is a steaming cup of peppermint cocoa. Mix a recipe of dry-ingredient cocoa, seal it tightly in a glass container, and pair it with a hefty mug. Wrap it all with wire-edge organdy ribbon.

Minty Hot Cocoa for You!

ayer the dry ingredients for Ultimate Brownie Mix in a vintage or new airtight jar. The gift recipient adds butter and eggs—and voilà! Tasty, warm brownies to take off the edge of a bitter cold day. Candy-coated chocolate pieces add festive color to this masterpiece.

Sweet stirrings—just like your favorite coffee shop serves. Chocolate-dipped spoons pair perfectly with the warm drink of your choice. Dip plastic spoons into warmed chocolate and drizzle with white chocolate—or reverse the chocolates for variety. Bundle a week's worth of choco-spoons into a bouquet and present them in a colorful cup with a saucer.

*E*veryone loves the bright, bursting flavor of blueberries. That's why blueberry scone mix is such a hit! Added to a vintage or new airtight jar, topped with a blueberry-blue tag, gingham ribbon, and faux berries, your scone mix promises tea party delicacies.

Hostess gifts abound with this selection of tasty munchies. Fill a canister to the brim with savory and crunchy cracker mix (above, lower left), seal it tightly and wrap a bow of raffia around the rim. A homemade blend of savory seasonings, tightly sealed in a decorative canister, will add zesty flavor to popped corn while watching a favorite holiday movie. Be sure to include a matching canister of popcorn—as well as a video copy of It's a Wonderful Life.

Italian Herb and Dried Tomato Risotto

Shown on page 149.

YOU WILL NEED

3½ cups Arborio rice
¾   cup snipped dried tomatoes
8   chicken bouillon cubes
3   tablespoons dried minced onion
2   teaspoons dried oregano
1   teaspoon granulated garlic
1   teaspoon dried rosemary
1   teaspoon dried sage leaves or dried basil leaves, crushed
½   teaspoon pepper

INSTRUCTIONS

Divide ingredients equally among four half-pint canning jars layering attractively. Add rice or dried tomatoes to fill small gaps, if necessary. **Makes 4 jars.**

GIFT TAG DIRECTIONS

Bring 3 cups of water to boiling in a large heavy saucepan. Add the contents of one jar. Cook and stir until boiling; reduce heat. Cover and simmer for 20 minutes (do not lift the cover). Remove from heat; let stand, covered, 5 minutes. Rice should be tender but slightly firm. Stir in ¼ cup freshly grated Parmigiano-Reggiano, Parmesan, or Romano cheese. **Makes about 6 (½-cup) side-dish servings.**

Minty Hot Cocoa

Shown on page 150.

YOU WILL NEED

1   10-ounce package mint-flavor semisweet chocolate pieces (1⅔ cups)
1⅔ cups nonfat dry milk powder
⅔   cup sugar
⅓   cup unsweetened cocoa powder
8   peppermint sticks or round hard candies (optional)

INSTRUCTIONS

Layer chocolate pieces, milk powder, sugar, and cocoa powder into 2-cup jars, dividing equally. Add chocolate pieces to jars to fill small gaps, if necessary. Tie a bundle of four peppermint sticks to the outside of each jar, if desired. **Makes 2 jars.**

GIFT TAG DIRECTIONS

Place jar contents in a large saucepan with 1⅔ cups water. Heat and stir over medium heat until hot and chocolate pieces have melted. Pour into four large mugs and serve with peppermint sticks or hard round candy. Top with ice cream, marshmallows, or whipped cream, if desired. **Makes 4 servings.**

Ultimate Chocolate Brownies

Shown on page 151.

YOU WILL NEED

1   cup all-purpose flour
½   teaspoon baking powder
¼   teaspoon salt
1½ cups Vanilla Sugar
¼   cup unsweetened cocoa powder
6   ounces candy-coated semi-sweet chocolate pieces; miniature chocolate-covered mint creams, quartered; any chocolate-covered candy bar, coarsely chopped; or a combination to total 1 cup
½   cup coconut, toasted nuts, or miniature marshmallows

INSTRUCTIONS

Vanilla Sugar. Fill a quart jar with 4 cups sugar. Cut a vanilla bean in half lengthwise and insert both halves into sugar. Secure lid and store in a cool dry place for several weeks before using. Keeps indefinitely.

Layer ingredients in a 1-quart canning jar. Tap jar gently on the counter to settle each layer before adding the next one. Add candies, nuts, or miniature marshmallows to fill small gaps at top of jar, if necessary. **Makes 1 jar.**

GIFT TAG DIRECTIONS

Combine ½ cup butter, melted and cooled, and 2 lightly beaten eggs in a large bowl. Gently stir in jar contents. Spread in a greased and floured 8×8×2" baking pan. Bake in a 350° oven for 35 minutes. Cool in pan and cut into bars. **Makes 16 brownies.**

Coffeehouse Chocolate Spoons

Shown on page 151.

YOU WILL NEED

6	ounces semisweet chocolate pieces
4	ounces milk chocolate pieces or white baking bar
20	to 24 plastic spoons

INSTRUCTIONS

Place semisweet chocolate pieces in a heavy saucepan over low heat, stirring constantly until the chocolate begins to melt. Immediately remove from heat; stir until smooth. Dip spoons into chocolate, tapping handle of spoon against side of pan to remove excess chocolate. Place spoons on waxed paper; refrigerate for 30 minutes to allow chocolate to set up.

Place milk chocolate pieces or white baking bar in a heavy saucepan over low heat, stirring constantly until chocolate begins to melt. Immediately remove from heat; stir until smooth. Place the melted milk chocolate or white baking bar in small, heavy self-sealing bag. Using scissors, make a small cut in the corner of the bag; drizzle one or both sides of the chocolate-coated spoons with the melted milk chocolate or white baking bar.

Refrigerate spoons for 30 minutes to allow chocolate to set. Wrap each spoon separately. Can be stored in a cool dry place for 2 to 3 weeks. **Makes 20 to 24 spoons.**

Blueberry Tea Scones

Shown on page 152.

YOU WILL NEED

2	cups all-purpose flour
1/3	cup Vanilla Sugar (recipe, opposite)
1/2	cup nonfat dry milk powder
2	teaspoons baking powder
1	teaspoon dried lemon peel
1/4	teaspoon salt
1/3	cup shortening that does not require refrigeration
1	cup dried blueberries

INSTRUCTIONS

Stir together flour, Vanilla Sugar, milk powder, baking powder, lemon peel, and salt in large mixing bowl. Cut in shortening using a pastry cutter or fork until mixture resembles coarse crumbs. Stir in blueberries. Place in a 1-quart canning jar. Tap jar gently on the counter to settle contents. Add dried blueberries to fill small gaps, if necessary. Store at room temperature for up to 6 weeks or in freezer for 6 months. **Makes 1 jar.**

GIFT TAG DIRECTIONS

Place jar contents in a large mixing bowl. Add 1 beaten egg and 1/4 cup water; stir just until moistened. Turn dough out onto a lightly floured surface and quickly knead by folding and pressing gently for 12 to 15 strokes or until nearly smooth. Pat to 1/2" thickness. Cut into desired shapes with a floured 2½" to 3" cutter, dipping cutter into flour between cuts. Place scones 1" apart on an ungreased baking sheet. Brush tops with milk, if desired. Bake in a 400° oven for 12 to 15 minutes or until golden. Transfer to a wire rack to cool slightly. Serve warm. **Makes 10 to 12 scones.**

Pesto Popcorn Seasoning Mix

Shown on page 153.

YOU WILL NEED

3	tablespoons butter-flavor sprinkles
2	tablespoons grated Parmesan cheese
1	teaspoon dried basil, crushed
1/2	teaspoon dried parsley flakes, crushed
1/8	to 1/4 teaspoon garlic powder

INSTRUCTIONS

Combine butter-flavor sprinkles, Parmesan cheese, basil, parsley flakes, and garlic powder in a small bowl. Give as a gift with unpopped popcorn. (Seasoning mixture will coat about 10 cups of popped popcorn.) Store mix in the refrigerator.

Cracker Mix

Shown on page 153.

1	cup bite-size fish-shape crackers
1	cup oyster crackers
1	cup bite-size shredded wheat biscuits
1	cup miniature rich round crackers
2	tablespoons cooking oil
1/2	teaspoon Worcestershire sauce
1/8	teaspoon garlic powder
	Dash bottled hot pepper sauce
2	tablespoons grated Parmesan cheese

INSTRUCTIONS

Combine crackers in a large bowl. Mix oil, Worcestershire sauce, garlic powder, and bottled hot pepper sauce in a small bowl; pour over crackers, tossing to coat. Sprinkle cracker mixture with Parmesan cheese; toss to coat. Spread mixture on a shallow baking sheet. Bake in a 300° oven for 10 to 15 minutes or until golden, stirring once. Cool completely. Store in an airtight container. **Makes 4 cups.**

CRAFTING BASICS

CROCHET

Chain One Stitch

Make a slipknot about 4" from the end of the yarn and slip the loop onto the crochet hook. Weave the yarn loosely under the little finger, over the ring finger, under the third finger, and over the index finger of your left hand; grasp the tail of the yarn between the thumb and third finger. Hold the hook (with the slipknot on it) in your right hand, slip it under the yarn; use the hook to pull it through the loop to complete one chain stitch. Continue chain-stitching the desired number of stitches to make a foundation chain.

Single Crochet

Step 1: At the beginning of a row, insert your crochet hook into the second chain from the hook.

Steps 2 and 3: Slip the hook under the yarn, and then use the hook to pull it through the chain. This is called "yarn over" (or "yarn over hook") and is abbreviated as "yo." Notice that there are two loops on the hook.

Steps 4 and 5: Yarn over again, and then pull the loop completely through the two loops on the hook. You have just completed a single crochet. To work the next single crochet, insert your hook into the next chain, and repeat Steps 2–5.

Double Crochet

Step 1: At the beginning of a row, slip the hook under the yarn (yarn over), and insert the hook into the fourth chain from the hook.

Step 2: Yarn over again, and pull the loop through the stitch. There are three loops on the hook.

Step 3: Yarn over, and pull the loop completely through the first two loops on the hook. Notice that two loops remain on the hook.

Step 4 and 5: Yarn over once more, and pull the loop through the remaining two loops on the hook. One loop remains on the hook. You

have just completed a double crochet. To work the next double crochet, yarn over and insert your hook into the next chain; repeat Steps 2-5.

Slip Stitch

Step 1: Insert your hook into a stitch. Yarn over, and pull the yarn through the stitch and through the loop on the hook. You've completed a slip stitch.

CROSS-STITCH

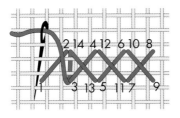

Basic Cross-Stitch

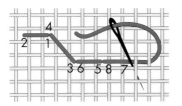

Backstitch

TRANSFERRING PATTERNS

Transferring a Pattern onto Fabric

1. Use an iron-on transfer pen with dark ink color for light-colored fabrics and white ink

for dark fabrics. Unless the pattern is printed in reverse, trace it with a pencil onto tracing paper, flip it over, and trace it with an iron-on transfer pen.

2. Position the tracing paper ink side down on the fabric. Using a hot iron without steam,

press on top of the paper to transfer the design.

Transferring a Pattern onto Wood

1. Duplicate the pattern by placing tracing paper over the design and tracing over it with pencil.

2. Transfer the design to the project surface by taping down the traced pattern. Place

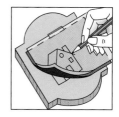

transfer paper under the pattern, and trace over it again with a stylus or pencil.

PAINTING

Stencilling

1. Dip the bristle tips of a dry stencil brush into the paint. Tap off

most of the paint on a paper towel.

2. Apply the paint to the surface by pouncing the bristle tips up and down to

create a fuzzy or textured look.

Shading and Highlighting

1. Select a main color, such as red, and use it to base-coat the surface. Apply paint with the

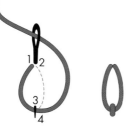

largest brush that will fit the design area.

2. Shade with a darker color, using the float-ing technique. Shading makes an area appear

to recede, separating it from the surrounding color.

3. Highlight your work by floating a lighter color on the design. High-lighting makes

an area appear more prominent, adding dimension.

STITCHES

Blanket Stitch

French Knot

Lazy-Daisy

Running Stitch

Satin Stitch

Stem or Outline Stitch

SOURCES

Look for supplies to make our projects at arts, crafts, fabric, and needlecrafts stores, or contact these companies for more information.

CRAFTS

Accu-Cut Systems (die-cuts),
1035 E. Dodge St., Fremont, NE 68025;
800/288-1670; www.accucut.com.

Accent Design (wooden cutouts),
3690 W. 1st Ave., Eugene, OR 97402;
541/485-1406.

Activa Products, Inc. (Celluclay),
P.O. Box 472, Westford, MA 01886-0012; 800/255-1910.

Art Accents (tiny holeless beads),
4208 Meridian #1, Bellingham, WA 98226; 877/733-8989;
www.artaccents.com.

Artistic Wire (colored wire),
725 N. Larch, Elmhurst, IL 60126;
630/530-7567; www. artisticwire.com.

Crafters Edition (wooden cutouts),
available at Joanne's Fabric and Crafts.

Darice Inc. (grapevine bows),
(no individual sales) 13000 Darice
Pkwy., Strongsville, OH 44149;
800/321-1494; www.darice.com.

**Decorator & Craft Corp.
(papier-mâché boxes),**
428 S. Zelta St., Wichita, KS 67207;
316/685-6265.

**Elizabeth Ward & Co., Inc.
(Blue Moon Beads),**
4218 Howard Ave., Kensington, MD
20895; 301/897-8311.

Foss Manufacturing (Kunin Felt),
380 Lafayette Rd., Hampton, NH 03843;
630/929-6100; www.kuninfelt.com.

**Inkadinkado
(rubber stamps and mini-grommets),**
61 Holton St., Woburn, MA 01801;
800/888-4652; www.inkadinkado.com.

**Personal Stamp Exchange
(rubber stamps),**
360 Sutton Pl., Santa Rosa, CA 95407;
800/782-6748; www.psxstamps.com.

**Provo Craft
(glass teardrops and woodturnings),**
285 East 900 South, Provo, UT 84606;
800/937-7687; www.provocraft.com.

**Red Castle Rubber Stamps
(rubber stamps and Fit It Volume I for
box templates),**
P.O. Box 39-8001, Edina, MN
55439-8001; www.red-castle.com.

**Suze Weinberg (Ultra-Thick
Embossing Enamel),**
www.schmoozewithsuze.com.

The Beadery (plastic beads),
105 Canonchet Rd., Hope Valley, RI
02832; www.thebeadery.com.

**The Little Fox Factory
(handcrafted cookie cutters),**
931 Marion Rd., Bucyrus, OH 44820;
419/562-5420;
www.thelittlefoxfactory.com.

Tsukineko (rubber stamp ink)
15411 NE 95th St., Redmond, WA
98052; 425/883-7733
www.tsukineko.com.

FLOWERS

California Cut Flower Commission,
Visit www.ccfc.org for flower arranging tips
and floral information.

PAINT

Binney and Smith (Liquitex paint),
1100 Church Ln., Easton, PA 18042;
800/272-9652

DecoArt (paint),
P.O. Box 386, Stanford, KY 40484;
800/367-3047; www.decoart.com.

Delta Technical Coatings (paint),
2550 Pellissier Place, Whittier, CA 90601-1505; 800/423-4135; www.deltacrafts.com.

**Duncan Enterprises
(Aleene's and Tulip paint products),**
5673 E. Shields Ave., Fresno, CA 93727;
559/291-4444; www.duncancrafts.com.

Krylon (spray sealer),
101 Prospect Ave. NW, Cleveland, OH
44115; 800/457-9566; www.krylon.com.

Plaid Enterprises (FolkArt paint),
3225 Westech Dr., Norcross, GA 30092-3500; 800/842-4197;
www.plaidonline.com.

**Ruppert Gibbon & Spider, Inc.
(Jacquard Textile paint),**
P.O. Box 425, Healdsburg, CA 95448;
800/442-0455 www.jacquardproducts.com.

NEEDLEWORK

Coats and Clark (Red Heart yarn),
Consumer Services Dept., P.O. Box
27067, Greenville, SC 29616;
www.coatsandclark.com.

DMC (embroidery floss and thread),
10 Port Kearny, S. Kearny, NJ 07032;
973/589-0606; www.dmc-usa.com.

Better Homes and Gardens.

CHRISTMAS

FROM THE HEART.

VOLUME NO. 10

Editor-in-Chief	Beverly Rivers
Creative Director	Daniel Masini
Editor	Nancy Wyatt
Associate Art Director	Carrie Topp
Contributing Graphic Designer	Sundie Ruppert
Editorial Coordinator	Carol Linnan
Editorial Project Coordinator	Barb Hickey
Contributing Writers	Karen Weir-Jimerson and Rhonda Matus
Administrative Assistant	Mary Johnson
Contributing Copy Editor	Debbie Smith
Contributing Illustrators	Glenda Aldrich, Barbara Gordon, and Chris Neubauer Graphics
Contributing Photo Stylist	Jill Abeloe Mead
Publishing Director	William R. Reed
Publisher	Maureen Ruth
Group Consumer Marketing Director	Liz Bredeson
Marketing Manager	Becky Nash
Business Manager	Kristen Eaton
Production Manager	Douglas M. Johnston
Book Production Managers	Pam Kvitne and Marjorie J. Schenkelberg
Vice President	Jerry Ward

Chairman and CEO	William T. Kerr
Chairman of the Executive Committee	E.T. Meredith III

Meredith Publishing Group

Publishing Group President	Stephen M. Lacy
President, Magazine Group	Jerry Kaplan
Corporate Solutions	Michael Brownstein
Creative Services	Ellen de Lathouder
Manufacturing	Bruce Heston
Consumer Marketing	Karla Jeffries
Operations	Dean Pieters
Finance	Max Runciman

For editorial questions, please write:
Better Homes and Gardens® Christmas from the Heart®, Vol. 10
1716 Locust St., GA 307, Des Moines, IA 50309-3023

CONTRIBUTING PHOTOGRAPHERS

Craig Anderson: Pages 66–67 and 71–79.

Scott Little: Pages 2–3, 5–12, 19–24, 27–28, 31–40, 44–48, 50–52, 57–58, 61, 65, 69, 81–88, 95, 101–103, 105–107, 112, 114, 124, 126, 128, 132, 138–144, 147, 149–154, and 159–160.

Cover Photograph: Scott Little

Printing Number and Year: 5 4 3 2 1   05 04 03 02 01

ISSN: 1081-4698

ISBN: 0-696 21364-8

At Christmas play and make good cheer,
    For Christmas comes but once a year.
            —*Thomas Tusser*
                c. 1524–1580